The Silent Traveller in Edinburgh

The Silent Traveller in Edinburgh

Chiang Yee

mercatpress
www.mercatpress.com

First published in 1948 by Methuen & Co
This edition published in 2003 by Mercat Press Ltd
10 Coates Crescent, Edinburgh EH3 7AL
www.mercatpress.com

ISBN: 184183 0488

Cover image: *The Castle in the Summer Haze*, Chiang Yee
Inside cover: *Courting on the Little Pond in the Royal Botanic Garden*, Chiang Yee

Set in Galliard and Marigold at Mercat Press
Printed and bound in Great Britain by Antony Rowe Ltd

Contents

THE SCOTT MONUMENT FROM WEST PRINCES STREET GARDENS

Illustrations

To the spirits of the Magnolia
in the Royal Botanic Garden

Foreword

The Silent Traveller series was popular in Britain during the 1940s. However, many people did not know or remember the name of the author, though they had read or heard of the pen-name The Silent Traveller. Thus, it was not surprising that a quiz published in the Edinburgh *Evening News* on 7 May, 1949 included the question, 'What is the name of *The Silent Traveller in Edinburgh*?' The answer was Chiang Yee.

When *The Silent Traveller in Edinburgh* was published on 18 November, 1948, Chiang Yee had already successfully established his reputation as a travel writer and artist. Beginning with *The Silent Traveller: A Chinese Artist in Lakeland* (1937), Chiang published *The Silent Traveller in London* (1938), *The Silent Traveller in Wartime* (1939), *The Silent Traveller in the Yorkshire Dales* (1941), and *The Silent Traveller in Oxford* (1944) as well as his Edinburgh book within a short span of ten years. Surprisingly, Chiang had come to England only as recently as 1933, with very little grounding in the English language. In addition to these six Silent Traveller books were twelve other English language books he published between 1935 and 1948, among which were a memoir, two introductory books on Chinese art, a work of fiction and several children's books.

Chiang Yee was born in 1903 in Jiujiang, an ancient city on the Yangtze River in China. He received a solid classical training in childhood at the family school and studied Chinese painting with his father, a well-known local artist. After graduation from the National Southeastern University in Nanjing with a major in chemistry, Chiang taught chemistry at middle school, joined the Northern Expedition to fight warlords and unite the nation, and then served as chief of three counties in Anhui and Jiangxi provinces. In 1933, Chiang left for England, where he taught Chinese at the University of London and then managed the Chinese collections at the Wellcome Institute of the History of Medicine. In 1955, he accepted the teaching position in Chinese studies at Columbia University and moved to the United States. During all those years, Chiang travelled extensively and left his footsteps almost all over the world, yet he was not able to visit his home in China until 1975, after an absence of forty-two years. During his second trip to China in 1977, Chiang was hospitalised in Beijing and passed away on October 17.

Chiang Yee's travel books had a distinctive style, remarkably different from other travel books, so much so that one could instantly identify them in a library or bookstore. Chiang designed all the dust jackets himself. Across the top is the English title in cursive script that the author penned with a brush. Under that is a colored painting and the Chinese title in calligraphy. On the book spine are the English title and the author's signature, again in a cursive script that is pleasant, unique and eye-catching. Chiang's creative energy and talent are evident to anyone who skims through or ruminates over those vivid descriptions of travel experience, interspersed with numerous beautiful colour plates, line drawings, and Chinese poems, executed in Chinese calligraphy, alongside their English translation.

Chiang Yee wrote thirteen Silent Traveller books, of which twelve have been published. The first six of these books, ending with the Edinburgh book, were about British locales; after that, Chiang wrote about other parts of the world. In the Edinburgh book, Chiang began with a review of his own creative work and delineated his theory on literary and artistic creation, defending his pioneering efforts and practices in exploring new subjects and technique.

Thousands of readers have been enchanted by the Silent Traveller books, which are refreshing, charming and enlightening. Common to these books are three appealing features which I would like to discuss briefly with examples from the Edinburgh book: defamilarization and reconstruction; profound simplicity; and the pictorial quality.

Chiang Yee loved to defamiliarise the world around him and transform a common scene into an unfamiliar sight or a normal concept into an abnormal one. For example, the author is transformed into 'an imaginary Scot', wearing the Great Plaid with a bonnet in hand. Likewise, Robert Burns, clad in Chinese robes, strolling leisurely with a folding fan in hand, is said to be a Chinese Confucian by birth. Moreover, Arthur's Seat, which has been traditionally interpreted by the Scots as being in the shape of a lion, is re-visioned as an elephant. Such an act of defamiliarisation is in essence a challenge to an established world order or a rigid belief system, and opens our eyes to new possibilities. It requires insight, courage and imagination. Yet defamiliarisation has never been the ultimate goal of the author; it is merely a necessary step leading toward a new vision and new understanding that the author brings to his readers through the reconstructed picture. Chiang proclaimed repeatedly that he intended to underline the common ground between East and West and to bring about a mutual understanding by writing and commenting on what he had observed in the West. Such reconstruction has allowed him to highlight those common features or characteristics shared, as in the present book, by both Scots and Chinese. He makes us aware that the elephant, associated with Arthur's Seat, is not just an animal well beloved in Asia; it is 'the most respected of animals' by the entire human race. He has made us aware that there exists some essential bond between the folk songs of ancient China and Robert Burns' poetry. He has made us aware that Chinese and Scottish people are similar, since he, of Chinese origin, could be mis-identified as an 'imaginary Scot', while an aged Scot could so resemble an 'inscrutable Chinese'.

Chiang Yee always observes the world around him with insatiable curiosity, exploring those seemingly trivial details and searching for some undiscovered meaning. His casual, conversational comments are often pleasant and charming, though they may appear superficial or sometimes even childish; nevertheless, it is not difficult to discover that they contain some profound philosophical ideas, often cloaked in simple observations. Seagulls, for example, have long been admired in China as a symbol of the 'gentleman of leisure', carrying soaring aspirations and being devoid of common vice or provincial traits. Unfortunately, as Chiang observes, modern consumer culture has exerted its negative impact even on these lovely birds, for they have given up their natural diet of fish in favor of the free food offered by pedestrians: 'The example of the effect of environment upon character urges me to be careful!' In another instance, Chiang is amazed by a small girl on the tramcar, who voluntarily returns the excess change to the conductress. In this honest, pure-minded little girl, Chiang catches hopeful glimpses of the future. The relatively long discussion that follows emphasises the need to enrich our spiritual life in the midst of material construction in the postwar world while affirming the hope of honesty, integrity, and freedom from excessive desires. According to Chiang, we humans have grown so sophisticated that we 'can no longer comprehend the clear child-mind.' 'World peace can last if we are able to keep our minds simple and our hearts pure.'

Finally, the pictorial quality in his travel writings is worth noting. Reading Chiang Yee's travel narrative is like appreciating art works. With good training in Chinese painting, Chiang possessed the gift of artistic sensibility that enabled him to be a keen observer and a skillful producer of beautiful impressionistic narrative text. Standing at the same vantage-point as other people, he seldom failed to catch some fascinating details or make some exciting discoveries that could have otherwise been overlooked. Natural elements, such as rocks, trees, clouds, water, mountains, birds and animals, were his favorite subjects in travel narratives. Those vignettes, intermingled with descriptions, comments, reminiscences, and anecdotes, were like details of scenes on the painter's canvas. Chiang understood that a true artist should go beyond the external appearance to seize the basic form and inner spirit in order to give a masterful representation of the subject. His descriptions of Edinburgh Castle exemplify this point dramatically. Chiang presents to the reader his impressions of the Castle from different perspectives and in various conditions: in sunlight, in the rain, at dusk, in the wind, or in the moonlight. These vignettes are simple word-pictures of everyday life and common incidents, rich in details, primarily focusing on the gradual unfolding of the author's surprises and ecstasies with his unexpected discoveries. When juxtaposed together, these impressionistic word-pictures generate exhilarating and poetic effects on the reader, very similar to Claude Monet's masterpieces, such as his Rouen Cathedral or Water Lilies series.

For Chiang Yee, Scotland held a special meaning because of Sir Reginald Fleming Johnston (1874–1938), Chiang's mentor, colleague, and friend. A Scottish native, Johnston had gone to Asia after graduation from Oxford and stayed there for over three decades. He served as district officer and magistrate in Weihaiwei, China, from 1906 to 1917. In early March, 1919, he became English tutor to Pu Yi, the last emperor of China who was dethroned in 1911. Much of Johnston's experience as the imperial tutor in the mysterious Forbidden City has been recounted in his fascinating memoir *Twilight in the Forbidden City* (1934). Recognised as an eminent scholar, prolific writer, and sinologist, Johnston was appointed director of the Chinese Department of the School of Oriental Studies (SOS) at the University of London in 1931.

In October, 1934, following an interview with Johnston, Chiang Yee was hired to teach Chinese as a lecturer at the SOS. Chiang admired Johnston for his broad range of knowledge and excellent understanding of both Western and Chinese cultures; likewise, it was a pleasure for Johnston to have a young Chinese colleague with whom he could share much of his interest in Chinese culture and have stimulating conversations. In 1936, Chiang, after passing the qualifying exam, was accepted as a doctoral candidate, studying Buddhism and then Chinese calligraphy with Johnston. Unfortunately, Chiang was never able to finish his Ph.D. study because Johnston resigned his post in June 1937 and returned to Edinburgh, where he died in March of 1938.

Johnston bought the island of Eilean Righ on Loch Craignish in Argyll as his residence in 1934. After retirement, Johnston invited Chiang Yee to visit his home on the island, where Chiang stayed for two weeks in late July of 1937. Chiang was at a crossroads, beset by worries and uncertainties in his career and personal life. He was not sure if he could continue to pursue and complete his Ph.D. study. He was not sure if he would be allowed to continue to teach at the SOS. He was not sure what was happening to his hometown and his family in China after the Japanese invasion on 7 July. Finally, he was not sure what the fate of his first Silent Traveller book, which had been accepted for publication by Country Life in London, would be. Yet Chiang's first visit to Johnston's home in the summer of 1937 allowed him a chance to appreciate the beautiful literary and art collections that Johnston had brought back from China. He enjoyed the idyllic scenery around him, where he floated freely in the boat on the mirror-like loch circumscribed by lofty mountains and where the mail service ran only once a week. 'It is quite out of the world,' wrote Chiang to his friend during his stay there. The trip gave him a temporary relief from the relentlessly oppressive difficulties in his life, and this experience must have become part of his fond memories of Scotland.

Chiang Yee once shared with a friend his firm belief in the value of life, 'I have been working diligently because I believe that a man leaves a name behind him just as a tiger leaves a skin behind.' To transcend the limits of time and space through art and literary creativity had been Chiang's persistent objective for over four decades, and he hoped that his contributions to art and literature would be appreciated and remembered by future generations. Today, half a century after their initial publication, Chiang's Silent Traveller books still retain their original freshness and vigor, appealing to new generations of readers and critics. Indeed, when reading these books, we feel as though we are accompanied by Chiang Yee, whose travel accounts and insightful comments help broaden our perspective, bring a new understanding of ourselves as well as the world outside, and remind us of the urgent need for cultural exchanges, mutual respect, and global co-operation.

Da Zheng
Boston, February 2003

i

Unnecessary Introduction

Each time I have striven to fix my impressions of travel in words and drawings and assemble the results in a book I have had to write an introduction. Is an introduction really necessary? I doubt it. But having written one for each of my other books, I should feel this one to be incomplete without an introduction. Here therefore begins the Unnecessary Introduction.

It is ten years now since I ventured to produce my first travel book, *The Silent Traveller in Lakeland*. After it had been rejected several times for publication I was kindly advised not to press for its appearance because my drawings were so utterly Chinese that no one would understand them and the book would find very few readers. For some reason this encouraged rather than disheartened me. The book duly appeared, and I have continued to send forth my travel impressions at intervals ever since. The results are not Chinese in any typical sense: they are the personal impressions of *one* Chinese, not of all Chinese.

Many readers have been interested enough in my humble work to want to ask me questions about it. Especially they ask why I call myself 'The Silent Traveller'. I do not always find it easy to answer. Once I caused laughter when I explained to the Mayor of Wakefield that I found the Yorkshire dialect very difficult to follow and that my part in conversations with people I met on the road could not go beyond 'Good morning' or 'Good evening'. Edinburgh citizens in particular and Scottish people in general would perhaps have understood that explanation! And anyway it is perfectly natural to be silent when one is travelling alone!

But this name of 'The Silent Traveller' did not originate with my travels in Britain. It is the literary translation of my Chinese pen-name, 'Ya-Hsin-Chê', which means 'Dumb-Walking-Man'. I chose this name for myself after I gave up my office of District Governor of Kiukiang, a post which combined the work of the chairman of a county council and a magistrate. Being thus a civil servant as well as being involved in local politics, I had been kept talking day and night for five years or so. This did not suit my temperament and I was glad to escape from it. From Confucius' saying, 'Don't talk too much; talking too much leads to trouble', and also from the poet Li Po's words, 'The Universe is the hotel for all Creatures', I composed my name 'Dumb-Walking-Man'. To the Chinese, only travellers or walking-men need accommodation in a hotel; human beings are regarded as one of the many types of creatures living in the hotel of the universe. In this sense 'The Dumb-Walking-Man' or 'The Silent Traveller' suits me very well, though 'Hsin-Chê' or 'Walking-Man' is often used as a term for a roaming Buddhist monk.

Many years have passed since I gave myself the name, and I have grown so accustomed to it that it is in the titles of some of my works. Many people now address me simply as 'The Silent Traveller' instead of by my actual name and surname, which I suppose is difficult to remember and to pronounce. I was once called by a Birmingham editor, who noticed that I do talk a little from time to time, 'The Not-too-Silent Traveller'.

The subject-matter of my paintings has been much discussed. Naturally I am free to choose it. Some of my readers seem to overlook the fact that, though a Chinese by birth, I have come to live in an environment different from that in which I was brought up. Being an artist, trained and interested in observing Nature carefully, I have not spent a period of years in Britain without making some record of my surroundings. My work cannot be expected to wear the conventional overcoat of old Chinese paintings. Nor do I feel that I should confine myself to being a mere copyist of old Chinese styles without any innovation or technical development appropriate to the times and circumstances in which I have been living. The consistency of Chinese art throughout the whole four thousand years or more of its history is one of the wonders of civilisation; but the weakness of the determination to carry on the long tradition as strictly as possible has become evident in the last three or four centuries. We have advanced very little. How then could I express myself, since I have absorbed so much that is alien to the Chinese mind?

However, unlike a Chinese cook, who can turn an English or a Scottish cabbage into a Chinese dish, I have definitely not set out to turn the British scene into a Chinese one. In my view there is no difference between the arts of the West and of China as regards beauty and artistic value: the distinction lies in differing techniques and media. Untrained in Western techniques and media, I have tried to interpret British scenes with my Chinese brushes, ink and colours, and my native method of painting.

We have two kinds of strokes, Kung-pi (fine strokes) and Ta-pi (big strokes) or Hsieh-i (writing a thought or painting a mood). Both are executed with brushes, and I use both according to my mood and the subject. The fickle weather in Britain which constantly changes the aspect of the scene stimulates me to record my own varying moods. My aim is not to produce a mere representation of the external appearance of my subject, but to seize its basic form and inner spirit, and to give these free expression without interference from abstract ideas. Whether I have ever achieved my aim or not I cannot say, but I am still pursuing it.

In technique I have encountered many difficulties. Taken singly, the trees, flowers, birds, mountains and streams in Britain are sympathetic to my brush, but to represent their grouping often needs much thought. Western architecture keeps me puzzling how best to render it. Often it takes me a long time to reach an even tolerably satisfying result. But I derive immense pleasure from my efforts and from exploring the scope of our media... the rather stiff brush with its fine point, the ink, and the soft, absorbent paper. The ink is a marvellous substance, with an unending range of tone, and it is always a joy to me to play with it.

Of course I hear all kinds of remarks about my work. Some people, interested in China and everything to do with it, exclaim with joy that they like it because it is by a Chinese; they usually add that I have turned the British scene into a Chinese one. Students and ardent lovers of our art regret that I have abandoned our age-old traditions for a 'degenerate' or 'hybrid' type of art. A few simply refuse to cast a glance at my work, because they consider it absurd that the British scene should be depicted by a Chinese. I listen and remember the following old Chinese story. A dwarf was sailing down the Yangtse when his boat was driven aground by a strong wind. He tried to help to push her off again, but his hand slipped and he fell into the water, which covered his head. When he emerged he shouted, 'Who said this water was shallow? I call it deep!' It is all a matter of opinion.

As to my written words, they only express my personal reactions and feelings towards the experiences which have come my way. Whether they give the right point of view or not, is not for me to judge; they are myself; I am not in a position to ask my readers to take my side. Nor have I any desire to *preach* what I believe.

A friend of mine once asked a man, who mentioned reading my books, whether he had actually met me or not. The man answered that there was no such person as 'The Silent Traveller', who was an imaginary character made up by an Englishman! If so, perhaps the experiences of Edinburgh described in the following pages were made up by an imaginary Scot!

IMAGINARY SCOT

COURTING ON THE LITTLE POND IN THE ROYAL BOTANIC GARDEN

ii

Misinterpretation

To be greeted on my arrival in Edinburgh by drizzling rain seemed to me an appropriate welcome. Not that I had come to Scotland for rain, but I did know that I should often meet this friend of mine in Scotland, and our immediate meeting made me smile. Edinburgh was a new place to me, though I had been in it once before. I had arrived in the dark one August evening in 1937 after a few days' stay in Callander and had not been able to find accommodation at any of the addresses provided by a friend, for the city was flooded with people attending the World Educational Conference, the World Christian Congress, or something of the kind. At last, with the help of one of the admirable Edinburgh policemen, I got a room for two nights at the Caledonian Hotel. The first night passed without incident. On the second night I was bewildered by the dazzling floodlight on the Castle, which left with me an impression of unreality, like a picture from a fairy-tale book, spurring me on to discover for myself the reality of Edinburgh.

For this second visit, in August 1943, I had made every arrangement before leaving Oxford. And here I must express my admiration and gratitude to the staff of L.M.S. Head

Office for their endless trouble in providing me with a sleeping berth after duly fulfilling the requirements of the Government. Their courtesy enabled me to start out happily on my journey. The chief happiness of travelling long distances in wartime is in reaching one's destination, no matter what weather one may find there, and when I came out of Princes Street Station and found the drizzling rain to dispel the drowsiness of the long journey, I felt that here at least were some facilities for washing my face, for such provision is not to be found in the trains in wartime. In China it is our custom to give a dinner welcome called 'Hsi-cheng', or 'Washing-off-the-dust', to a friend arriving from a long distance, and although, naturally, I could not expect such a dinner on my arrival in Edinburgh, the rain certainly did try to wash off the dust from my shabby clothes.

En route for Marchmont Road, my taxi drove through the Meadows. The broad expanse of bright green carpet which had given me such pleasure in the London Parks seemed here to lend a faint tint to the rain-lines, as if the sky were breathing on them a greenish vapour. I have always loved fresh green because it has both life in itself and the power of blending other colours. It is unfortunate that no pigment will retain this valuable quality for long, and I wish passionately that I could discover how to retain its freshness in my work.

Green, it seems to me, is the principal colour in Nature. Black and grey may predominate in winter and the brighter colours in spring and autumn, but green is with us the whole year round. Could a single red or yellow flower be beautiful without its background of green? And is it not a real joy to see, after a long, bleak winter, leaves of tender green on the trees? It was sheer delight to me after my journey to see this soft green in rain. Yet I remember that in 1934, when I had not been long in this country, an English friend bought a green motor-car, and one member of his family could not bear to look at it because of its colour. Liking the colour so much myself, I was amazed to meet someone who objected to it, and wondered whether there were perhaps even people who wished to abolish green in Nature.

When I awoke from my day-dream I was at my destination. I installed myself at my digs, had a meal, and strolled along to the post office in Strathearn Road to despatch a telegram. It was raining heavily by this time, and I had no intention of beginning my sight-seeing yet, but when I reached the post office I suddenly caught sight of the hazy outline of a grey-blue hill behind the distant roofs and tree-tops. It looked so near that I was tempted after all to make its acquaintance immediately, so I crossed over to Beaufort Road and walked steadily along the narrow road, craning my neck eagerly. But as I skirted the high walls of buildings the hill disappeared from view. It was not until I approached the church of St. Catherine's-in-Grange that it revealed itself again, its outline dim through the thick rain-lines. Its shape seemed familiar, and I paused. Yes—that was it! A tortoise! A huge, motionless tortoise; the rocks, though their outline was softened by the rain, resembled a very strong shell. I recalled to mind Kuei-shan, 'Tortoise Hill', in the centre of Kiukiang, my birthplace, where in my childhood I spent many happy hours flying kites, and I wondered if, on fine days in peacetime, I should have seen children flying kites on this Scottish hill.

From the broad Dalkeith Road, with the hill now fully in view, I was amazed at the deceptive power of space. Standing near the closely packed houses, with little to create an illusion of distance between my eyes and the hill, it had seemed near, rising between two tall trees as a perfect blue silhouette against the grey rainy sky. Now, away from the buildings, and with a clear view of the hill, it appeared further away than before! My faith in the power of *space* in Chinese pictorial art grows stronger as my own experience increases, and once again I realised how clever were our Sung masters in their exploitation of it, particularly in landscape painting. They knew that when an artist puts on to his canvas every detail that comes within his orbit, his picture is cramped and seems to cry for breathing-space; whereas if certain objects are omitted in favour of space, the composition of the work acquires balance both realistically and imaginatively.

THE ELEPHANT-HILL

But now as I reached the end of Park Road joining the direct path to the hill, the shape of the hill had changed. It was no longer a tortoise but—a sitting elephant! The rock on my left was the head, and the sloping hill adjoining it the long trunk. Outlines were sharp and clear, though it was now drizzling again. We have in Chinese a phrase 'ling-lueh'[1] which means 'to accept into the understanding', and I endeavoured to 'ling-lueh' the beauty of the formation of the crags, the rocks, the hill-tops, and the winding paths. Tranquility reigned, yet everywhere there was life, unfettered, proud, the spirit of dour determination, and industry, for which the Scots are so justly famed. Yet, in spite of their majesty, the hills seemed to smile at me as if they had been already acquainted with others of my race. I felt my friendship was an ancient and trusted sentiment, and I was happy.

1 See *The Silent Traveller in Lakeland*, p. 23

The scene was changing swiftly, and Nature was demonstrating her magic powers. Volumes of white mists rose, layer upon layer, forcing their way through two gaps where footpaths lead to unknown paradises, and threatening to encircle the hill and engulf the whole landscape. Soon the valley was filled with mist. On my face I seemed to feel the light, friendly touch of the small white particles, coming singly in play to touch my face and dart away again. Then they jostled me in small groups: had I stepped back a pace? What a pleasant sensation it was! The obvious analogy came to mind: how a great united effort of all mankind would obliterate certain evils that resist stubbornly our isolated efforts.

Soon there were neither crags nor rocks nor footpaths, but the elephant-hill was still visible. The elephant's ears were small, and I felt proud of myself for actually knowing that it was an Indian and not an African elephant. Thus are we vain of our paltry knowledge! My elephant appeared to have been lifted by the mist to a higher position; it sat there in ease and content, oblivious of the waves of mist madly chasing each other in all directions, its small eyes refusing to be troubled. I have often wondered at the biological make-up of the elephant; at the contrast between its huge body and small eyes; and its contented mind.

He seemed at last to grow tired of sitting, so for a time he floated steadily along the ocean of mist, and then squatted on top of the waves, like 'The Flying Trunk' in one of Hans Andersen's fairy-tales, though this trunk was not made of wood! I chuckled as I thought what an admirable title for my elephant 'Flying Trunk' would be!

Later in the day I bought an Edinburgh evening paper and read about 'Arthur's Seat', which it appeared was the name of the rock on the hill I had seen that morning. I learned with horror that I had completely misinterpreted the shape of this hill and rock, for the Scots have always seen them as a lion. But then I remembered reading in Buffon's *Natural History*:

> The human race excepted, the elephant is the most respected of animals... Every being in nature has his real price, and relative value; to judge both in the elephant, we must allow him at least the judgement of the beaver, the dexterity of the monkey, the sentiment of the dog, and to add to these qualifications the peculiar advantages of strength, size and longevity... To this prodigious strength he joins courage, prudence, coolness and an exact obedience; he preserves moderation even in his most violent passion; he is more constant than impetuous in love; in anger he does not forget his friends; he never attacks any but those who have given him offence; he remembers favours as long as injuries... he is not naturally an enemy to other animals; he is beloved by them all, since all of them respect him, and have no cause to fear him.

I felt comforted, for I had not gained, and am not now giving, a wrong impression of Scotland by misinterpretation!

iii

False Competition

There were many quiet roads near my lodgings, though when setting out for a walk I usually took the nearest one. The Robertson Memorial Church (formerly Grange Parish Church) with its tall spire and clock was always the first thing that met my eyes as I came out on to Marchmont Road. I had never been inside the church, but one day I found myself walking along the footpath through Grange Cemetery. Reflecting that there must be some famous people buried there, and many interesting tales relating to them which I, a foreigner from a country thousands of miles away, could not know, my thoughts wandered off at a tangent.

I have often pondered on the capacity and limitations of human memory. Think, for instance, how many names and events I have to remember in the four thousand years of my country's history. It is bad enough to have to remember my own ancestors living a hundred, or even a thousand years ago: now I have to remember not only these, but names and events of many other countries as well! In spite of strenuous efforts I find it very difficult—and I am sure that any Britisher in China must find the same—to learn, and sometimes even to pronounce, the names of many of the renowned personalities

ST GILES' IN THE RAIN

I have come across in my travels. Yet we seem to expect each other to remember these things as a matter of course. The capacity of our memory ought, it would seem, to be perpetually increasing, yet it has a limit, and when that limit is reached some things must be forgotten in order to make room for others.

Now that we are all crying out for better international understanding in the post-war world, we shall have to remember still more about each other. Is it possible for us to do so? New personalities arise, and new events take place, every day. How I wish I might have lived in the simple days at the beginning of human history! The next generation will have more to remember even than we have, and may even envy us! We can at least lessen their burden by not adding to the names which will occupy the limited space in their skulls. Yet look at those who struggle to 'make a Name', and the many who worship a Name. Their number increases every day as the result of modern methods of publicity. Men do not consider how short and unimportant is their stay in this world, nor stop to ask whether others have room in their heads to store their names. I am glad that at least here in the West I can still choose what to remember and what to forget, with the excuse that I am, after all, a Chinese.

All these reflections had been set in train by the sight of the gravestones in Grange Cemetery. The people buried in the cemetery had probably never even wished to be remembered after death, though they could not prevent others from revering and remembering them. They certainly would not have expected an almond-eyed person like myself to visit them. So I hurried away from the cemetery.

I walked on down Kilgraston Road. There was nobody in sight. The morning air refreshed my mind, and the appearance of the sun made a pleasant change from the two previous days. I crossed to the other side of Oswald Road, and was turning to the right when I was stopped by two Americans in uniform who asked the way. I could not tell them, and they went on, roaring with laughter. I did not know what they were laughing about, but it must have been something in the sense of the old Chinese jest about 'asking the way of a blind man'. I chuckled to myself too.

I passed through a gate and stood for a while by a pond at the foot of Blackford Hill. Here I noticed a girl of about thirteen, with another much younger girl and a boy of five or six, sitting on a public seat on the other side of the pond. I wondered why they did not come down and stand by the water's edge and feed the birds, like the children by the Serpentine in Hyde Park. Three swans and a few ducks floated idly about, and did not appear to feel neglected. Another part of the pond was dotted with white seagulls which did not utter a single cry or scream—different again from the London parks. As I called to mind those familiar rancorous cries for food the present scene breathed an unusual and almost unbelievable tranquillity. I thought how every creature plays its part in the life of Nature, and what varied moods and feelings Nature engenders in her disciples. No doubt I myself at that moment, in the imagination of the children, and perhaps even of the birds too, was playing my part in a very different scene.

Those few white seagulls on the little pond led my thoughts away again. I do not remember seeing many seagulls in my younger days, for my home town is far inland, but I have read of them in many of our great poems. Two lines of a poem by a famous Sung poet, Huang Ting-Chien (A.D. 1105), still ring in my ears, though I was only thirteen when my old tutor, after describing the scene they depict, used to chant them to me. Here they are:

To the South of the river the
  open water is even greener
  than the sky;
Over there is a white seagull,
  as idle as I am!

江南野水
碧於天中
有白鷗閑
似我

黄庭堅句

He used to tell me another story about a well-known scholar called Li Fang (A.D. 925-996). In Li Fang's garden were five birds, each of a different species, whom he called his special guests. There were a heron—'guest of snow'; a stork—'guest of immortality'; a peacock—'guest from the South'; a parrot—'guest of majesty'; and a seagull—'guest of leisure'. The seagull has always been in our literature a symbol for the 'gentleman of leisure'. Though I accepted this symbol, I had no proof of its aptness in my later travels in the neighbourhood of Shanghai, Tsingtao, Hong Kong and Hainan Island, and still less when I met those clamorous seagulls in London. I even began to doubt whether the observations of our literary men were accurate, for we Chinese are not considered scientifically minded people. Now at last I saw that I need never have doubted. The white seagulls dotted about the little pond were quite at ease. The quacking of the ducks did not make them turn their heads; not even the ripples on the surface of the water disturbed them. They showed no trace of greed or of any other common vice. They could float on the pond or fly away at will. Were they not truly 'gentlemen of leisure'? You may argue that the swan also lives a leisurely life, but to that I would reply that the swan is no gentleman, but a snob; his long, haughty neck and fierce eyes betray it.

I must admit, however, that not all seagulls are gentlemen of leisure, for certainly those to be seen in London parks are not! After all, the busiest city in the world is hardly a suitable place for a gentleman of leisure: the temptations and enticements of money and vanity are too great. In London the seagull develops a lust for the food offered him, even abandoning his natural diet of fish for crumbs of dry bread. This example of the effect of environment upon character urges me to be careful!

Our poets of old could not have known that seagulls inhabited the towns, for they would surely not otherwise have chosen this bird as their symbol for 'a gentleman of leisure'.

From my little knowledge of London social life, I should compare the London seagulls to the glamorous girls who frequented big social gatherings in pre-war London, with their amusing ephemeral chatter; while the seagulls near Blackford Hill are like provincial beauties of quiet, unsophisticated charm. The modern urge towards internationalism tends to kill every form of provincialism. For artistic value and for beauty I prefer to retain 'provinciality' and local colour. I therefore cast yet another look at the seagulls near Blackford Hill.

BLACKFORD HILL

After walking a few steps up the footpath I left it for the soft grassy slope of the hill. As I climbed higher the ripples on the pond below disappeared, and the seagulls became tiny white dots, until at last the pond became like one of those oval mirrors so often found on the walls of European houses, and the white dots the collected dust of months (due, I reflected with a smile, to the war-time lack of domestic service).

From where I stood, half-way up the hill, I could see the top of the Castle as well as the top of Arthur's Seat. Suddenly

I was smitten with a childish desire to compete with Arthur's Seat as to which of us would stand the higher from the top of Blackford Hill. I was only mildly discouraged by the fact that Blackford Hill seemed much higher than Arthur's Seat, which was further away. I turned and climbed the hill backwards, with my eyes fixed on Arthur's Seat. It seemed to keep pace with me, though at the same time it seemed that we were both standing still watching the houses and trees that smiled below us. Eventually both houses and trees vanished in the mist, while Arthur's Seat rose prominently in perfect outline in the distance. I felt annoyed with myself for having for a moment supposed that from Blackford Hill I could look down on it as on a small point on an embossed map.

I continued to climb backwards, however, trying to reach a still higher vantage point, until I collided with a boy who dashed out suddenly from behind a gorse bush. I grasped his arm to prevent his falling, and he smiled and said, 'Sorry, sir'. Two younger boys standing by the bush, who had apparently been playing hide-and-seek with the eldest, roared with laughter at our collision. When I greeted them they became shy and hid behind the bush. I explained to the first boy why my back had been turned to him and asked him if he had ever thought of doing such a thing. He looked puzzled, declaring that he knew Arthur's Seat was higher than Blackford Hill, and I began to feel I had been behaving like a silly grown-up. A child might walk backwards up a hill just for the fun of it, but without any idea of competing with another solid hill. We grown-ups tend to assume that we know all about the child-mind: actually our own minds have become so complicated and confused that they can no longer comprehend the clear child-mind: but whether silly or not, I enjoyed my own private competition with Arthur's Seat.

The three boys had run down to the bottom of the hill while I was at the top. I wondered if they were discussing with each other all the queer things they had heard about the

Chinese and their inscrutable ways. But probably this was only another piece of my adult-sophistication.

The next people to appear were a man and woman with a little girl of four or five. An elderly man followed them to the Direction-Indicator and pointed out several places. The little girl was told to stand by the Indicator, and her father prepared to take a photograph of her with the elderly man. Suddenly a gust of wind blew the child's hat away. She stretched out her arms after it as if she too were going to fly away; they all laughed and ran after the hat, and I saw them no more. I was curious to know whether a photograph had actually been taken at the precise moment when the hat took wing. Then I looked at the spot they had chosen for the photograph. Modern photography is good for close study of an object, but very seldom reveals any feeling of height or depth. There could never be the same feeling in a photograph taken from where I was standing as in the actual view below me. Every object was covered with a huge feathery carpet of white mist. In the distance Arthur's Seat remained stately and tranquil. Although I knew it was not very far away, the mist gave me the illusion of great distance. I remembered the view of Inchkeith in the Firth of Forth which I had seen from Calton Hill on a clear day. But Arthur's Seat, unlike the island, which had given an impression of distance and not of height, seemed to have been lifted far up into the sky above the sea of mist white touched with purple. Wondering at this tinge of colour it suddenly occurred to me that—of course!—it was just the time for Scottish heather to be in bloom, and that perhaps the slopes of Blackford Hill might be covered with it. The mauve vapour might be breathed out by the heather and tinting the mist. Red is a hot colour and blue a cool, but purple is warm and tranquil, and the city was bathed in warm tranquility.

I lingered here a long while. A white seagull fluttered high above my head keeping me company while I composed this poem:

The steep rock squats like an elephant;
But the Scots see it as a lion.
How generously it floats in the air,
Its ancient face full of valour and courtesy.
The houses are lost in the mist;
A lonely bird is playing in the wind.
Leisurely wandering with no single thought in my mind,
I stand to gaze round, regardless of time.

巉石蹲如象
蘇人呼作獅
憑虛何曠逸
古貌足威儀
萬戶雲中失
孤禽風裡嬉
逍遙無一念
佇看不知時

遠望愛丁堡獅子山咏

iv
Unexpected Informations

I have always felt sympathy with the views of our great Sung poet and essayist, Su Tung-P'o, in the enjoyment of pleasure wherever it may be found. About a certain building in China, Chao-Jan-Ting, he wrote that there must surely be some charm in everything, and, that being so, we should find pleasure in any experience, however small, and not be for ever looking for the exceptional. Again, he said: 'Those in search of happiness and avoidance of trouble, find that happiness brings both pleasure and trouble, unpleasantness or sadness. But human desires are unending and the things which fulfil them are limited, and there is always the risk of bad being mingled with good. Consequently one is continually in a quandary whether to accept satisfactions. This leads to less enjoyment and more unpleasantness, and the seeker may find that he is really looking for trouble and rejecting happiness. This is contrary to human nature!' Of course it is; but it is unfortunately true that the mind of man is often in conflict with itself without being aware of it. Those who anticipate do not always get what they expect. I—and there are probably many like me—who have never bothered to anticipate, usually find pleasure in all sorts of unexpectedness. My first Sunday morning in Edinburgh offered proof of this.

As I mentioned before, I arrived in Edinburgh in a drizzle, and the same night there was a heavy thunderstorm. I was too tired after the journey to wonder whether I should be drenched on my wanderings next day, and in any case, during the few years I have spent in this country I have never complained about walking in the rain. I have in fact explained on more than one occasion in my other books how my affection for rain increases each time I behold a familiar scene take on a new and enchanting aspect through a veil of rain. I am no immortal, however, and when it rains my clothes become as soaked as those of other mortals. It would seem that the rain becomes fonder of me as time goes on, for it invariably follows me on my travels in this wet country. There is certainly plenty of rain during the year in most parts of the British Isles, and perhaps Scotland gets more than its share, I cannot help feeling, in this connection, that the rain has done at least one good turn to the Scottish people in making their cities, towns, and even their little villages much cleaner than those of other parts of the British Isles. In spite of my apprehension it was, after all, fine and sunny when I awoke in the morning. A sunbeam stole through the crack between the window and the blackout curtains and shone straight on to my bed. My feeling for rain by no means prejudices me against sunshine, for which I have a great affection, particularly when it arrives thus unexpectedly.

After a quick breakfast I got ready for a long stroll. I have never been in the habit, as most visitors have, of reading a guide-book first and then working out a plan. I prefer to 'ling-lueh' whatever crosses my path. I may waste much time in getting to some noted place which could easily have been reached with the help of a guide-book, or I may even miss altogether a number of well-known sights. No matter: it is my way of travelling.

BURNS' MONUMENT IN STORM

Edinburgh is a capital city, but it is unlike London. It is also a city of learning, but unlike Oxford. I expected to see, on Sunday morning, a quiet city without bus or train service, as in Oxford. Here was another surprise, for as soon as I left the house I found trams running to and fro. Why? They were, it seemed, carrying passengers to church. In the short time since my arrival I had noticed several churches in the neighbourhood of my lodgings, and from its many spires and towers I imagined that Edinburgh must have as many churches—I should say 'kirks'—as Oxford.

I found I could now either take a train or walk along by the tramway through the Meadows to Princes Street, but the fresh green of the Meadows after the rain eliminated the alternative. My eyes were dazzled and my feet came to a halt. Amid the freshness that surrounded me I felt the life pulsating in my veins. To my left, a little above the houses, rose the faint outline of the top of the Castle, and to my right, behind a group of trees in the distance, under the purplish veil of the sun-streaked morning mist, rose the massive yet graceful hill known as Arthur's Seat. This was not what I had expected in a capital city: instead of hurry and bustle I was enjoying clear air and a pleasant sense of solitariness.

Presently I found myself walking towards Forrest Road. In front of me I noticed a crowd of people converging from all directions upon a path through the Meadows. Apart from a few in uniform, most of them were either elderly or very young. Nearly everyone carried a Bible, and they walked with the assurance of people who know their objective. Although I am not a Christian I was moved by these signs of genuine faith.

The crown of St. Giles' Cathedral was visible in the distance. I recognised it, for it had been pointed out as an object of interest by a policeman of whom I had asked the way to the Police Station, where, in accordance with wartime regulations, I had gone to report my arrival. I assumed that the crowd was on its way to the Cathedral now, but it was not. Most of the people disappeared into small churches on the way. A group of five, probably on holiday, emerged from a side-road and hesitated at the door of Tolbooth Church, which was still closed. Balked of entry they walked on in the same direction as I. I have been told that the Scottish are a deeply religious people, and after that Sunday morning I can well believe it.

From Bank Street the massive building of St. Giles', with its crown and tower dominating the city, was most impressive. Edinburgh High Street is not as empty on a Sunday morning as Oxford High Street. I had spent a little time looking at both an old square brick well and the fine statue of the Duke of Buccleuch, when my attention was arrested by a crowd of people streaming through the main entrance of the Cathedral. I must confess to an imperfect knowledge of the Scottish language, but I believe the Scots speak of 'the Church *skailing*' when referring to a stream of people pouring out of a church-door. Having attended many church services, I might have entered the Cathedral had I not been attracted by the Mercat Cross, and as it was still early I crossed over to get a closer look.

'That's the auld Edinburgh Mercat Cross', a rough but friendly voice said unexpectedly in my ear. I turned to see an elderly gentle-man who had apparently crossed the High Street on purpose to give me the information. He wore a weather-beaten cap, underneath which his hair showed white at the temples. The many deep lines running down his cheeks announced him as a man of experience and maturity, while his huge bristling white moustache, nearly hiding his nose and mouth, reminded me forcibly of a man whom I had met in my childhood, some thirty years before, when my sister had taken me one Sunday to see her Missionary School. He was a foreigner with just such a huge moustache. This had impressed me, probably because Chinese rarely grow large moustaches, and for a long time I imagined that every Westerner had one. Indeed, there was some years ago a fashion among British people to wear such moustaches. I had lived in this country for a good many years, seldom encountering a huge moustache, and the vivid memory this one produced gave birth to a nostalgic longing to be with my sister again after so many years' separation.

My companion told me that he was one of the oldest citizens of Edinburgh, though he had spent most of his life abroad, chiefly in the East. He had been in Hong Kong, Shanghai and Hankow some fifty years ago. Mention of Hankow brought back that feeling of nostalgia, for it stands above my native city of Kiukiang on the upper Yangtse River. No one can go by boat from Shanghai to Hankow without passing Kiukiang; and I told my friend that he had passed my birthplace before I arrived in the world. I have heard that one cannot make a Scot laugh except by reference to incidents of his childhood, and this was borne out by my companion, for he roared with laughter. Having been born in China, I could not possibly imagine what a Scot might have done in his young days, but for some reason I had provided this old citizen of Edinburgh with a good laugh.

MERCAT CROSS

I have found many characteristics common to both Scots and Chinese, one of which is surely the so-called emotionless expression that Westerners always say they find on Chinese people. We have even on occasion been caricatured as not very distinct from apes! Certainly the wrinkles and weatherbeaten appearance of this old man's face gave him an air of inscrutability. It seems to me that a plain countenance is preferable to a perpetual meaningless smile. If we Chinese do have something to laugh about, we can laugh as wholeheartedly and genuinely as this old Edinburgh citizen and I were laughing now.

Presently my new acquaintance asked me where I had come from and whether I was sight-seeing. I answered that I had just come from Oxford. He admitted that there were many interesting things to see in Oxford, but was quite sure that there were still more in Edinburgh. To whet my appetite he told me that, many years ago, on kings' birthdays and other high festivals, rivers of red wine used to flow at this very cross. He then commanded me to follow him to the statue of Charles II and pointed out details of great interest in the sculpture of the horse, which was made of lead. Next he took me to a brass sign which marked John Knox's grave in Parliament Square, once a graveyard. Seeing a few Americans in uniform walking round the Parliament Buildings reminded him that he had heard there were descriptions of Harvard on one of the doors, so we went over to look for them, but in vain. He remarked that these Americans seemed to know everything about Edinburgh, and I suggested that this must be because of their Scottish ancestors. He laughed again. In following ancestral traditions and in their eagerness to learn about their ancestors, the Americans are not very different from the Chinese.

Having been brought up in Confucian respect for my elders I was touched by the kindness of this old man who was so anxious to show me the old part of the city, and I followed him closely. First we went to Riddle's Court, which, he told me, was the house of a very rich merchant of the sixteenth or seventeenth century, who on many occasions gave banquets to King James VI and his Queen. The house had a double courtyard, which nevertheless was not as large as the courtyards of my home in China. The inner sanctuary had an air of seclusion, which was possibly the reason why those royal personages chose so often to leave their Castle and seek recreation within the walls of Riddle's Court.

I was astonished to hear of such an unusual connection between the King and a rich merchant. In China, some two thousand five hundred years ago, the social position of a merchant, whether rich or poor, was put very low by Confucius, who held that the ruler of a nation should concern himself directly with the right conduct and happiness of his subjects, and must therefore be surrounded by upright scholars and wise men. In Confucian teaching a merchant's thought must always focus on 'gain', which might be won by either rightful or wrongful means, not necessarily by his own labours, but by his exploitation of the services of others. Such conduct of life without the spirit of self-sacrifice could hardly serve as an example to the ruler of the nation. On what idealistic lines our forefathers' minds were trained! How many of our rulers in the long history of China ever put their ideals into practice? If our minds had not been directed into this highly idealistic channel, we might have achieved a better practical system of carrying out our duties honestly. As the standing of a merchant was so low in Confucian society, no ambitious person cared to take up such a career, but tried instead to be a scholar. Unfortunately these were of many types, only the minority being upright and wise. Even among scholars the rich seemed to hold a more important place in society than the poor, and so it is perhaps not to be wondered at that most of them were not content until by hook or by crook they became some kind of government official. This led to China's unfortunate reputation of possessing a corrupt official class and accounts for her slow progress in industrial and scientific enterprise. The Second World War has taught us to broaden our minds, and the future of my country looks to be bright and hopeful.

VIEW OF THE OLD UNIVERSITY AND 'SCOTSMAN' BUILDING FROM NORTH BRIDGE

At this stage of my long meditation I unconsciously smiled. My acquaintance imagined that my smile was in acknowledgment of the story he had just told me, so he related some further anecdotes. Then we visited a few more closes, including Lady Stair's Close, where I was persuaded to walk a little way up the turnpike stairs. It was so dark inside, that I found this difficult. This experience suggested to me the reason why in Britain some means of lighting, either by gas or paraffin or electricity, have eventually been found out. On turning back my companion showed me the bronze marks of the old prison wall on the road in the High Street, the Heart of Midlothian, and a brass sign like a capital 'I' on the spot where the last criminal was executed in public in Edinburgh. He told me that the only person at that time executed 'in camera' was a Frenchman (I did not catch the name) who poisoned his wife. He also declared that he himself was probably the only living person with any knowledge of this event, since the Frenchman had taught in his school. He must have taken me for a keen historian! But I did not disillusion him: I smiled and said nothing.

Through a gap in the High Street facing the Scott Monument my informant said it was possible on a very clear day to see the Firth of Forth. That day unfortunately was misty though the sun was shining. Presently he bade me goodbye, and turned for home before I could thank him properly. Unexpected friendliness of this kind in a city new to me had warmed my heart greatly, and my belief in the goodness of human nature was therefore strengthened. What interested me most about him was that during all our time together he had been smoking the butt of a cigar fixed on to a penknife. I was fascinated by this, for it verified the stories I had heard about the Scots' economical way of living. Many people treat these stories as a joke, but I admire the Scots for their thrifty habits, which indicate that they have a sense of the comparative value of things. I am sure that most Scots have found little difficulty in complying with wartime restrictions. This is another characteristic in common between the Scots and the Chinese, for we too understand the principle of thrift.

After my friend's departure I felt inclined to wander further. I went in the direction of the Castle, and turned to the right down the long windings of Ramsay Lane. After my first acquaintance with Old Edinburgh the effortless descent was quite a relaxation. I knew I must some time go up to the Esplanade for a bird's-eye view of Edinburgh, but I postponed that for another time. On I walked contentedly, noticing little of consequence until I reached Ramsay Garden, which is a garden no more. I caught a glimpse of some interesting stone carvings on a door of nearby Ramsay Lodge. They were three decorative scenes—of carpentering, brick-laying and harvesting—well carved on stone or brick. From these subjects I got some idea of what appealed to the Scots. I particularly liked the harvesting scene, perhaps because I myself come from an agricultural country.

I next found myself on the Mound, looking down into the hollow which shelters the National Gallery of Scotland and the Royal Scottish Academy. Suddenly a shrill singing drew me towards West Princes Street Gardens, where I found a crowd of people listening to a boy of eight or nine who, on a stage fitted on each side with a loud-speaker, was singing hymns. I was impressed by the innocence and sincerity of his voice, which was so clear and penetrating that it drowned all other sounds. I joined the circle and silently sat down. I was handed a sheet of hymns. After the singing had ceased, a speaker stepped forward and gave a talk for the youngsters. Though I am no longer a youngster I am young enough to imbibe new knowledge, so I sat through the whole talk, listening carefully. Often I missed the meaning of single words, sometimes of even a whole sentence, owing perhaps to the speaker's accent, which it was difficult for me to follow. He was a somewhat stout personage. I could not see his face clearly from my seat, but though it was not for me to assume that he was on good terms with Scottish ale and whisky, his gestures and exuberance certainly suggested such an acquaintance. When he stretched out his arms I noticed that the youngsters sitting in front of me threw their heads backward a little; when he drew his fists to his chest they craned their necks forward. They seemed like puppets worked by strings in his hands. He spoke well and movingly. First he told of the meeting of Christ and Lazarus; after a while his talk turned to China. Surely, I thought, he has not seen me and altered his theme on my account? How could I restrain myself from listening even more intently to what he was saying about my country?

His story was that some forty or fifty years ago the head of a certain Christian Mission held a meeting in London at which he explained fully and urgently the need for missionaries to go to China to help the grievously suffering people there. Throughout the meeting not a single volunteer rose from the audience to offer himself for this task. The speaker—a Scot I assumed—went home depressed and shut himself in his study. At dusk his little daughter peeped through the keyhole and saw her father kneeling in prayer before an image of Christ. She opened the door quickly and declared that she had decided to give her life to God and to help in the work of which he had spoken. Her father was overjoyed and they knelt together in prayer. Presently the young son also came, peeped through the keyhole, and seeing what his sister had done opened the door and offered his own services. After a while sister and brother went to China to work for the Mission, and no doubt saved some of our souls!

The speaker told the story well and I was happy to have heard it. It even seemed possible that the priest I had seen at my sister's Missionary School had been this very boy, and the headmistress the boy's sister. I wished I could remember their names.

On my way home I tried to reason why in old days people used to dislike going to my country. I remember reading in Marco Polo's *Travels* that in the thirteenth century the great explorer's father and uncle were sent by our Mongol ruler, Kublai Khan, as ambassadors to the Pope 'to make a request to His Holiness that he would send a hundred men of learning, thoroughly acquainted with the principles of the Christian religion, as well as with the seven arts, and qualified to prove to the learned of Kublai Khan's dominions by just and fair argument that the Faith professed by Christians is superior to, and founded upon more evident truth than, other faiths'. Marco Polo also says: 'Kublai Khan moreover signified his pleasure that upon their (Marco's father and uncle) return they should bring with them, from Jerusalem, some of the holy oil from the lamp which is kept burning over the sepulchre of our Lord Jesus Christ, whom he professed to hold in veneration and to consider as the true God'.

No missionaries came to China at that time, however, and I am still puzzled as to why China has not received Christian thought more widely than she has. Although I am not a Christian myself I have read some Christian writings during my sojourn in this country, and have been continually struck by the similarity between the teaching of Confucius and Christian thought. Confucius, of course, was not a religious leader in the Western sense of the word. His followers did not hold religious services, but they were taught the principles of benevolence, virtue, the grace and refinement of a gentleman, decent conduct in life, and veneration of elders and ancestors. Are not these things Christian principles too? I have always thought that Christian teachings would have found a warmer reception in China than any other form of religious thought, had we and our Christian teachers not had preconceptions in our minds about each other's 'barbarous' nature. In China neither Christian scholars nor Confucian scholars have, until recently, made any direct contact with each other. The difference in language may have been too big a barrier for mutual understanding. My own view is that Confucius was too rationalistic in his teaching, not realising how his ideas would keep us bound within the limited framework of a family community, so that we have not developed a universal spirit for the benefit of the rest of mankind. This weakness in his teaching might be remedied in some way by Christian thought. I would like to see a solid body of both Christian and Confucian scholars studying together, and discussing their views without prejudice. The results of their combined efforts would surely bring good, not only to my country but to the world. But, alas, how can we do away with each other's prejudice?

THE STEEP STEPS

V

Ingenious Focalisation

Edinburgh Castle has a place in the heart of every Scot, even of those who have never lived in their native land. I wonder why this is so? There surely must be some other reason besides the Castle's position and the part it has played in the country's history. Being no geographer I cannot claim that, given a map of Scotland, I could locate Edinburgh immediately; nor, being no historian, am I the man to discuss Scotland's history from the Chinese point of view. Nevertheless, during my stay I not only began to understand the deep attachment of every Scot for Edinburgh Castle, but came myself under its spell.

Several Scottish writers and historians have told me that the origins of the Castle's history are lost in the mists of antiquity, and have added, as a point of interest, that the saintly Queen Margaret of Scotland lived there in the eleventh century A.D.—a period corresponding to the middle period of our Sung Dynasty (A.D. 960-1276). Native of a country whose history goes back some four thousand years, I instinctively trace things to their origin. I like to imagine the time when Edinburgh was covered, as was the rest of the present world, by the immense waters of the ocean. Centuries later, when the waters receded, it is my belief that the Castle rock and Arthur's Seat emerged before the surrounding land. On these promontories, wild beasts and human beings fought for their existence. In the course of time man perhaps sought protection from the savage attacks of these prehistoric wild beasts; and what better refuge could they have found than the Castle rock? By and by some of the cleverest of these forefathers of the Scottish race must have evolved a method of piling up big stones, until a primitive fortress was built; then rebuilt; until at last there arose on this rock what is now Edinburgh Castle.

I have no idea when the first castle-like fortress was built, but I like to imagine that it was at the same time as our Chinese forefathers built the fortress of the Great Wall, in the second century B.C. If you feel compelled to argue with me about the chronology of this supposition, I reply that since both races—Scots and Chinese—are similarly in existence at this moment, I see no reason why one should be further back in antiquity than the other. The only evidence, so far as I know, is that the Chinese have found earlier records than the Scots. You may ask me, too, why those Scottish forefathers did not seek protection on the top of Arthur's Seat and build the Castle up there. Perhaps they did build something of the kind. But from the look of the land surrounding that promontory there were perhaps dense forests situated there, full of wild beasts from which man sought to escape. All this, however, is entirely based on my own imagination, though such an ancient origin might serve to explain why the Scots are so much attached to Edinburgh Castle.

On the other hand, this affection might be explained on present rather than past grounds. Edinburgh Castle provides a wonderful spectacle both to those who live near and to visitors. It is kindly, and attracts people to its friendly walls. It has become the focal point for Edinburgh and its surroundings; there is no avoiding it; and one never tires of it, for it changes with every change of weather. I myself was enchanted with it and have never seen it look the same twice from any angle.

As I have mentioned before, I saw the Castle floodlit one night in August 1937. Although the effect was impressive, the Castle lacked its natural grandeur and beauty. I felt that, however many times one's acquaintance was renewed, its effect would never vary, and I did not regret, therefore, that wartime conditions prevented my seeing the floodlighting again. Nature remains unchanging: it is man who makes havoc of the world.

I have wandered round the Castle both at close hand and at wide range, and on the whole I find it most attractive from a distance. Let me describe some of my impressions.

One fine day, after a round of the pool, flower-beds and greenhouses in the Royal Botanic Garden, I found myself on the top of the highest rock in the Rock Garden. It was lunch-time and there were few people about. The distant spires and towers of the kirks, and the roofs of many high buildings, faded into the gentle hazy atmosphere. It was one of Scotland's perfect summer days, not too hot, and ideal for walking. Everything breathed peace and contentment. The sky was not blue, and thick clouds hung high above me. Suddenly I was dazzled by a shaft of sunlight that pierced the gilt-edged clouds and fell directly on to the Castle. It seemed almost like daylight 'floodlighting', and I imagined someone operating the lighting behind the clouds, as in a theatre. This light, however, was not artificial; it filled my eyes with its soothing golden light, and my whole being was warm with its radiance. The spires, towers and tall buildings around the Castle faded and lost their significance, but the Castle itself grew visibly in grandeur and stateliness. The sunbeam hovered there, the clouds, as though awe-stricken, retaining their distance. How could such splendour and radiance be perpetuated by brush and canvas, or any mechanical device? It must remain in my heart.

On another occasion I had a totally different impression of the Castle. I had climbed the rear slope of the hill in the Zoo Park near Corstorphine, and was resting on the summit. It was a beautiful sunny day and the sky was spotlessly blue. This was such a rare phenomenon to me that I did not expect it to last long. Sure enough, a few small woolly bunches of cloud soon appeared here and there in the blue vastness, looking very decorative. They moved about, some joining to form a huge perpendicular mass just above the Castle, over which it cast a dark shadow. The Castle was revealed in curious and gigantic contrast to the surrounding buildings in their bright insignificance. I amused myself by comparing the white mass to a canopy or vast umbrella spread over some African chief sitting in the scorching sun. The Castle looked calm and cool, and imbued me with its freshness after my hot walk up the hill.

I always liked the look of the Castle in the rain, but the occasion I remember best was one morning when I went for a walk on Braid Hills and saw it from Blackford Hill. After crossing Braid Burn to Blackford Hill and passing the signpost on the highest point of the latter, I sat down on one of the seats for a rest. My view lay directly towards the Castle, which stood clearly before me under the usual grey Edinburgh sky. Soon it began to rain, at first in big isolated drops, then in close vertical lines. I did not move. The shining streaks of rain pursued each other to the ground. The sky suddenly turned very dark and the Castle vanished from sight. After a while it became bright again—brighter than before, and I rediscovered the Castle, seemingly far away from me. We were separated by the myriad thick rain-lines, and through this transparent water-screen the Castle became elusive, and dazzling as if sparkling jewels were set in its grey stone. I doubt if such a startling effect could be reproduced artificially. It seemed as though the Castle were moving backward and forward all the while; when the rain slackened and the rain-lines thinned, it seemed to advance; when the rain was heavy and its lines thick, the Castle withdrew. What was still stranger was that when a strong wind blew the rain-lines diagonally, I thought for a moment the Castle had been blown away with them. But when the wind dropped it was still there, shining and gleaming, until a gust of wind from another direction carried it off again. Surely this Castle is the plaything of the Immortals, I told myself on my way home.

On yet another day, when a gale was blowing, I saw the Castle from Arthur's Seat. Who could correctly forecast Edinburgh's weather? It changes, not within a day or an hour, but within a minute. On this particular day I was sitting on a rock some way down the hill, facing the city. I was enjoying the view in leisurely fashion, and thinking idly, even dozing now and then, lulled by the mild air of a Scottish summer. I had even for a few restful moments forgotten my constant worry over my family far away in my long-suffering homeland. I was suddenly roused from my drowsiness by a strong gust of wind, the prelude to a gale blowing up behind me from the Firth of Forth. Within a few minutes it was howling round my back like the simultaneous whinnying of thousands of horses with, at the same time, a shouting battalion of infantry trying to seize the rock on which I sat. My thick black hair stood upright on my head and my coat-tails flapped. But I was not in the least perturbed, and determined to stick to my seat until something happened. Soon the gale attacked me with fury, but although rather shaken, I managed to hold on without yielding. The gale raged like a battle in front of me. Its divisions seemed to succeed one another, sweeping on easily, and moving forward without opposition. The spires, the towers and the tall buildings vibrated before my eyes, but the Castle stood solid, undaunted by the encircling onslaught. At that distance I could see very clearly the gale's furious rushes, and the menacing mass of clouds above the Castle. The battle raged, and the Castle did not flinch, but seemed rather to grow in magnitude. Who could fail to be inspired by such an indomitable spirit? As I watched I felt, not like a king, nor like a hero whose castle is besieged, for I had never desired to be a hero in any military sense, but just like one of many kindred souls who admire steadfastness in face of evils and difficulties. My own spirit was roused, and I knew that to overcome the difficulties with which I have to wrestle, and to reach the happiness which I know all human beings can achieve, I must stand firm and solid like the Castle rock. I arose in gratitude and lifted my hand to salute the Castle.

By now the gale had dropped and a gentle wind seemed to want to carry me over from Arthur's Seat to the Castle rock. I stretched my arms as if to embrace the Castle!

'There will be bright moonlight for ye tonight', said the lady of the house one evening when she came in to collect my supper dishes. This made me reflect on selfishness, that great weakness of human nature. It is a fault I always try to stifle, but it is not easy to detect, and even less easy to stifle when detected. I cannot help liking the Scottish phrase 'for ye'. To a Scot it means 'for you'; to me it means 'for me'. I could scarcely restrain my pleasure at the forecast that there would be moonlight *for me*. No sooner was I out on Marchmont Road than I became aware of the demon of selfishness creeping into my mind. I felt that the moonlight was for me alone, and I did not want anyone else to share it. The pairs and groups of people in Princes Street Gardens and in the Meadows were only making use of the moon and obviously not on intimate terms with her, so I decided to accompany her myself from the end of Radical Road along Salisbury Crags. No noise of traffic penetrated there and everything was at rest. The air was very clear and the moonlight of such white purity that I felt cold. It is strange how one's sensations change with one's surroundings, for had I been in China I would have welcomed that cool moonlight on a hot summer night.

The moon and I walked on together in perfect harmony, until at last I sat down to rest. A couple passed me, laughing, and I felt disturbed. How selfish I was growing! After this one interruption I was left alone with the moon as my sole companion. There was no vibration in the shadowy grass at my feet. Distant spires and towers were completely obscured by the massive darkness, save for the castle perfectly silhouetted in the moonlight, like an enthroned queen in a black velvet gown with a wide spreading skirt, with spires and towers for her courtiers making obeisance to her. There was dignity, honour and nobility of spirit in the tense silence.

'It was indeed for me', I said to the lady of the house when I returned. At first she did not know what I meant, and laughed, but before wishing me good-night she murmured, 'I hope there will be a fine day for ye tomorrow too'.

There is a small rock near Dugald Stewart's Monument on Calton Hill where I like to contemplate at leisure. I have sat there at all hours of the day, and in all weathers. I have enjoyed most of all the view of the Castle in the early morning and at twilight.

Nature is our great-hearted and compassionate mother. Instead of revealing her true form to us, she has her emissaries in every part of the world, and in Edinburgh her emissary is the Castle. The Castle and its rock from a distance are, to me, like a seated lady in an old-fashioned dress. She gets up very early in the morning and busies herself before anyone is about. Slowly she lifts the feathery bedcover of white early morning mist from the town and rouses her children—the good, and the not so good—and packs them off to work. At dusk they are tired and drowsy, so she spreads a darker bedcover of evening mist over the town, and her children prepare contentedly for bed, while she sits watching until all is quiet. She knows, of course, that her children are all very different. Some obey her implicitly; some are only too willing to indulge a little in drink, and some around Princes Street Gardens are perhaps very

CALTON HILL

wicked indeed! But all things adjust themselves, so she does not worry, for is she not the emissary of our broadminded mother!

At this very spot on Calton Hill I had another memorable view of the Castle at sunset. I had been sitting there for some time with bowed head, trying to recall some lines of a well-known but momentarily forgotten Chinese poem. They flashed into my head very suddenly, and in my elation I rose to my feet. At once I was met by a magnificent view of the Castle against a red, mauve and purple sunset reflected from the direction of the Forth Bridge. Clouds, like shining bars of gold, focussed their sparkling light on to the Castle, which looked like a queen in royal purple. Slowly, as I watched, the clouds turned into deep red, floating across the sky like great red goldfish, while the Castle queen reviewed the wonderful pageantry. The air was warm, intoxicating and jubilant. I dared not move until that radiant splendour sank first into deep purple and at last into intense black.

I can find no better way of taking a closer look at the Castle than to stand a few steps behind the Allan Ramsay statue after coming down from the Floral Clock, where I have found myself on many occasions. One very sunny afternoon, just after lunch, I took a walk along Princes Street Gardens and halted at this spot. There were a good many people about, but no one seemed to hurry lest he would disturb the tranquil atmosphere—or perhaps it was the drowsy air that retarded their movements? My eyes felt too heavy to open wide enough to see the Castle at all clearly between two big trees close by the road. Though the whole body of the Castle was within my view, the contours of the buildings were obscure, and faintly pale as if eager to mingle with the same grey-blue colour of the sky, an effect probably due to a very thin layer of greenish-tinted vapour rising from the many trees close round the Castle rock, screening the Castle and producing an infectious drowsiness in my eyes. The Castle rock is naturally dark in colour and harsh in texture, but now it seemed to become pale, gentle and soft under the summer haze.

People lay about on the slopes below it. Not a single leaf was moving, and the occasional seagull circling down only emphasised the stillness. The women's brightly coloured jumpers, and the flash of snowy-breasted gull, compensated for the lack of many flowers.

The scene was so enchanting that I decided to paint a picture of it.

Presently I continued my walk along the footpaths skirting the rock, and crossing a small bridge over the railroad I found myself in front of Ross Fountain, from whence I got a different view of the Castle. Here there were few people lying about, but I watched with interest a large flock of seagulls by the rock. A few more circled down to fill a gap in the centre of the flock. I was struck by the fact that the two sexes were not so obvious in their affections as certain human beings in other parts of Princes Street Gardens.

A LARGE FLOCK OF SEAGULLS

I was just about to go through a side-gate into Johnston Terrace when an elderly lady stopped to tell me something that seemed to amuse her a good deal. I could not altogether understand her, but I noticed a number of people round us craning their necks towards the rock, so I followed suit. I saw an old uniformed keeper struggling painfully, step by step, towards a huge boulder, behind which were two youngsters, one a girl in a red jumper. No sooner did the old man draw near than the young people moved still higher and were lost to sight. Another guard, standing at the foot of the rock, shouted to them to come down, but without success. Finally he called to his companion to leave them for they would have to come down in time. The sympathy of the watching crowd was obviously with the young adventurers, who had certainly, for the moment at any rate, won the day.

This incident added to the probability of the truth of a story I had read not long before. One dark and stormy night in March 1314, a soldier named Frank of the army of Sir Thomas Randolph of Strathdon, leading thirty men, had apparently crawled up precipitous cliffs through a howling wind and lashing rain to overpower the English garrison. He had been chosen for this job, so the story goes, because he had once been stationed at the Castle and had found a way of scaling the Castle rock to enable him to visit his sweetheart in the town below. What unimagined results had sprung from this romance! Romance as well as war can make people incredibly daring and courageous. There are many similar incidents in our history. After all, the history of all lands is closely connected with romance. Human beings, despite superficial differences in facial structure, language and dress, have the same romantic passions all over the world. Only in modern civilisation has romance been deprived of its colour. The two young people on the rock turned my mind to the fanciful dreams of my youth. What a nuisance the old guard must have seemed to them!

As I walked along Johnston Terrace I gave the Castle many a look until I turned into Chambers Street for a meal at the only Chinese restaurant in the city. As I ate I reviewed all my glimpses of the Castle, and felt certain that it was its ingenious focalising power which so attracted the Scots to it. Had I not myself been unable to withstand its spell?

vi
Mental Intoxication

One morning I felt restless and could not make up my mind what to do. It seemed a pity to sit indoors while much of this fascinating city of Edinburgh was still unexplored, but I felt lazy and my legs declined to move. As I pored over the newspapers, words and phrases such as 'War', 'Peace', 'Trapped', 'Captured', 'Biggest raid yet' and 'Alert sounded' started a disagreeable train of thought. My heart is not made of iron, nor am I an immortal free from earthly worries, and every day I was reminded by the news in the papers of my remote enemy-occupied homeland and of the conditions in which my family has lived for the last few years of war. How many thousands of people there must be who are even more anxious than I.

I have often succeeded in subduing such anxious thoughts by recollecting the happiest moments of my childhood and of my silent travels, so now I stretched myself out on the sofa and concentrated on visualising my wanderings in Edinburgh during the previous few days. Though I remained physically tired, this effort succeeded in refreshing me mentally, and I eagerly opened one of the five books on Edinburgh that I had bought the day before from a second-hand shop near

George Street. By degrees the speed of my reading slowed down, owing to the frequent appearance of such puzzling terms and expressions as 'Butter Tron', 'bonny bairn', 'built his *goose-pie* villa', '*Wallace* Cradle', 'warm study of daills' and 'the Sair Sanct'. Naturally I cannot read English as quickly as Chinese, and I had only the vaguest idea of the meaning of these expressions. They are not even to be found in the Pocket Oxford Dictionary I usually carry with me, and I came to the conclusion that the book must have been written solely for Scottish readers or for those well acquainted with the country. Although it was interesting to read the history of the Castle and the Royal Mile, I was somewhat discouraged by so much local dialect, and picked up the second of my five books. But here I was confronted with the same difficulty, and yet again in each of the remaining three, although I found much else to interest me. I was particularly struck by the different interpretations given by various authors of a particular event. How to decide who was right? And what of the future? If two or three Scottish historians had not been able to agree on a local historical event, how can one expect the historians of many nations to agree on the shattering world events of the last few years? It was beyond my comprehension. I threw the books down and went out to queue for some food, comforted to think that the desire to satisfy hunger, at any rate, is felt equally by all men.

Presently a clock in the neighbourhood struck three, reminding me forcibly that the day was half over—for I seldom heed the time when I am on my wanderings. I found I was now in the West Port, in olden days a vital point for the defence of the town. I did not know for how long the curio-shops along West Port had existed, but from the appearance of their shelves and windows I guessed they had stood there for at least two centuries. I wondered if the Scottish nobility, literati and wealthy people had frequented these shops as in China they had frequented those in Liu-li-chang in Peking (now Peiping). Liu-li-chang has for centuries been famous for its many curio and second-hand shops. For the last hundred years, as a result of the craze among the more sophisticated society of Britain and the Continent for 'chinoiserie', it has been known to almost every Western visitor to Peking, and indeed many Westerners went to Peking with the sole object of visiting Liu-li-chang. Although this bric-à-brac of fans, china and ornaments was not in any way representative of Chinese craftsmanship, it did succeed in rousing interest in our works of art in the West, and one might honestly say that the curio-shops along Liu-li-chang have made some contribution towards mutual understanding between East and West. The shopkeepers were well aware that the visitors from the West were their best customers, for they were less discriminating and knowledgeable than their own countrymen.

As I gazed at the windows of the West Port curio-shops, for it has always been a joy to me to spend an hour or two in such shops, I thought happily that I was probably the first foreigner to have found a Liu-li-chang in Edinburgh. As I entered one shop the owner, an elderly lady, rose from a low chair and said, without waiting for me to speak, 'Naethin' faur ye, sar, all oot'. Not understanding the rest of the sentence, I hastily glanced at a few small objects, thanked her, and departed.

The old man in the next shop I entered was anxious that I should take an interest in some little ivory carvings, known as 'Netsuke', made chiefly in Japan but sold as Chinese curios. Many London curio and art dealers make this mistake. Some years ago, when shown some ivory carvings, I pointed this out both to the dealer and to an English friend who accompanied me, but they branded me as a modern young Chinese with no knowledge of his own country's artistic accomplishments. I was careful, therefore, not to upset this cautious *auld* Edinburgh shopkeeper, and smiled (as I hoped) enigmatically. Eventually I came away with a half-crown brass medal bearing on one side a portrait of Queen Victoria. It resembled one I had bought for a shilling in the Caledonian Market in London seven years before, which I had lost in the bombing in 1940. The history of the medal was unknown to me, but I felt curiously sad that a hard-won medal could, after many years, be sold so cheaply to a casual customer.

From Grassmarket I paused to look at the Castle. The view was surprisingly like that shown on an early British water-colour I had seen, said to be a sketch by Paul Sandby made in 1751. From King's Stables Road and Johnston Terrace I climbed up numerous stone steps to the Esplanade, where I used to go for a wonderful view of Edinburgh. Today, after my climb up the narrow steps, the panorama seemed more gigantic than ever. 'Take the bitter first, then the sweet becomes sweeter!'

I joined a queue of people moving slowly into the small Chapel of St. Margaret, the oldest roofed building in Scotland. Near the door an elderly keeper in uniform was explaining something, but I did not understand his quick Scottish speech. Instead, I tried to recollect what I had read about St. Margaret that morning. The story goes that on the 16th of November 1093 Queen Margaret died of a broken heart after the death of her husband on the battlefield. Through a thick white mist—called by later Scottish writers a 'Miraculous Mist' and attributed by them to the saintly character of the Queen—both her coffin and her orphan children were carried to safety out of reach of the dead King's brother, whose intention of murdering his nephews and placing himself on the throne was known.

The thing that has most interested me during my silent travels is the common element between the legends and habits of my own country and those of other lands. The trifling differences necessarily existing have never seemed to me either interesting or significant. There are, for instance, many ancient

ADVOCATES' CLOSE IN TWILIGHT

Chinese legends telling of the escape of important historical personages in similar miraculous circumstances; and of similar tragedies of violent quarrels in royal families. Such things have occurred only too often in successive dynasties, despite the strict teachings of Confucius concerning human conduct. We have a legend very like the legend of the Scottish Queen Margaret. Chu Yuan-Chang, before he became the first Emperor of the Ming Dynasty, was defeated by a powerful opponent at Kiukiang in 1360 and retreated to the top of my beloved Lu mountain, just avoiding capture by escaping under cover of a heavy white mist. A monument has since been erected on the mountain-top. In my young days my elders and my nurse used to relate this legend, adding the explanation that, Chu Yuan-Chang being destined to become the Emperor, the Heavenly Lord had sent down the white mist to protect him. The parallel of the saintly Queen Margaret is striking.

THE ESPLANANDE FROM THE MAIN ENTRANCE OF THE CASTLE

Just then I noticed a circle of people outside the Chapel listening to an old guide. Another man approached the group, but the guide, saying that his talk was intended for a particular party, sent him away. I was surprised at such behaviour, but thought it wisest to remove myself also.

Another line of people were waiting to see the Scottish National Memorial of the First World War, and I joined on. This Memorial is a beautiful piece of work and does the artists credit. Nevertheless, I had a queer feeling about this spacious hall in its new dress. Perhaps it was too new to show up the grandeur and dignity of the War Memorial. I tried to visualise the place as the ancient palace hall where the treacherous 'Black Dinner' was held on the 24th of November 1440. On that day the Earl of Douglas, his only brother and their old adviser, Sir Malcolm Fleming of Cumberland, had been invited to a banquet in Edinburgh Castle. None of their retinue was admitted. During the feast, at which the young King James II and his Court were present, a *black bull's head*, said to be the ancient Scottish symbol of doom, was set on the table. The warlike young Douglases instantly sprang up and drew their swords to defend themselves, but were soon overpowered by the armed men who had been hidden in the banqueting hall. The three were executed for treason on the Castle Hill after a form of trial. I knew nothing about the actual trial, but I was struck by the fact that much the same thing had occurred many times in the ancient history of China. How many times has it already happened in our own day, in the great hall of Hitler's Berchtesgaden, where he has given banquets for Hacha of Czechoslovakia, Laval of France, and many another?

THE ROCK IN THE WAR MEMORIAL HALL

Many of the 'Black Dinner' plots in China's history are well known to us through our historical operas performed in theatres throughout the country. I shall never forget the masterly acting, particularly by the actor playing the part of Hsiang Yu, of 'Hung-Men-Yen' or 'Banqueting at Hung-Men', to which my father took me when I was thirteen years old. This banquet took place in about 207 B.C. after the fall of the Ch'in Dynasty; both the King of Western Chu, Hsiang Yu, and the King of Han, Liu Pang, determined to become Emperor of all China. One day Hsiang Yu invited Liu Pang to a banquet at his headquarters at Hung-Men. The plot was carefully prepared. Only one of Liu Pang's aides-de-camp, Fan Kwai, was admitted to the hall, and he stayed close to his master. During the feast, Hsiang Yu's officers, who were the real instigators of the plot, signed to Hsiang Yu to kill Liu Pang. Hsiang Yu hesitated, for he respected Liu Pang and was loth to be concerned in such treachery, and his officers themselves sprang up to do the deed. Liu Pang managed to escape, and subsequently, after defeating Hsiang Yu in battle, became the first Emperor of the Han Dynasty. Hsiang Yu has been called an infamous person in Chinese history, yet on this occasion he behaved heroically.

I next visited, in another part of the Castle, what was said to have been Queen Mary's apartments and the Crown Room. Owing to wartime conditions perhaps, I saw no tapestries of green brocaded velvet, no cloth of gold bearing the arms of famous princes and stories of classical, scriptural and mediaval personages, no chairs of gilded leather and damask. Even the Scottish Regalia, that crown of unknown date whose ancient golden diadem was set with rubies, sapphires, diamonds and big pearls, had been removed. The rooms were empty save for two old maps, one of Edinburgh and one of the Castle, hanging on the wall, and two glass cases containing an assortment of clay pipes and small coins. Women visitors, balked of the interesting relics, consoled each other in whispers. I myself did not linger long.

As I came out of the door a fellow-countryman of mine entered, accompanied by a stout and dignified Scot in a tartan kilt and two other friends. Before 1942, when China had not yet officially become one of Britain's allies, I rarely ventured to speak to a stranger with a similar flat face to mine, but now we greeted each other, exchanged names and a few words, and passed on. He was Mr. T. L. Wang, a Chinese engineer, who had come for a day's visit to Edinburgh from Manchester. He was the only Chinese I had met since I came to Edinburgh, and his stout companion was the first Scot I had seen there in a tartan kilt.

I sauntered out and leant against the low wall on the terrace. Many people were lingering round 'the great iron murderer', Mons Meg. Visitors had scratched their names on the seven other guns—another practice in common between our two countries! I was not very interested in the guns, but, unperturbed by the incessant chatter of the people round me, was absorbed in guessing from what point the Duke of Albany, brother of King James III, had escaped by rope down the jagged cliff. The Duke had been imprisoned in the Castle under suspicion of treason and he had only one more day to live when, with the help of a faithful groom of the chamber, he succeeded in escaping. He procured two bottles of French wine, which he presented to the Captain of the Guard and the three soldiers on duty, all of whom became drunk and were thus disposed of. Then he lowered the groom of the chamber by means of a rope. This unfortunately proved not long enough, and the groom fell and broke his thigh. The Duke lengthened the rope, lowered himself to the ground, and carried the groom on his shoulders for two perilous miles to Leith and safety. His courage and loyalty to the groom deserve the highest praise, but whether his escape was right I am in no position to say.

What interested me about the story was the bottles of French wine! Wine seems to have been an important element in intrigue. I could also find endless occasions in Chinese history where it assisted materially in the evolving of plots. I am not aware that it is known who, for his own ends, first employed wine to cause insensibility, but it is evident that both in the East and the West has been exploited for this purpose. Wine is supposed to have been made in China as early as five thousand years ago. When the great legendary Emperor Ta Yu first tasted it, he found it good, but quickly foreseeing that it would cause trouble, he put a ban on its manufacture. This, however, proved useless, and from that time wine was used for many a base purpose. Yet few refuse an invitation to drink wine, for, despite its potentialities, what magic power it has! I am sure the Duke of Albany has been by no means the only one to make good use of it in the past. I wonder whether in the Second World War any one of those who managed to escape from the hands of the Nazis did so with the assistance of wine? General Giraud, for instance: perhaps he knows only too well the possibilities in his country's wine and will never tell his story of escape!

ESCAPED BY ROPE DOWN THE JAGGED CLIFF

ARTHUR'S SEAT IN THE MORNING MIST

Rousing myself at last, I saw a half-moon already high in the sky, though it was not yet five o'clock. When I first came to Britain I used to be startled to see the moon while there was still bright daylight. I remembered a poem composed by Li P'o on his visit to Soo-Tai:

In the deserted pavilion of the
  old palace the willows are still
  new,
But spring becomes unbearable
  while listening to the song of
  the gathering of water-caltrop.
Above there is now only the
  moon over the Western river
Which has ever shone on the
  occupants of the palace of the
  king of Wu!

舊苑荒臺楊柳新
菱歌春唱不勝春
只今惟有西江月
曾照吳王宮裡人
李白蘇臺覽古詩

The last line is explained by the fact that the most renowned beauty in Chinese history, Hsi-Shih, was one of the occupants of the palace of the King of Wu at the beginning of the third century before Christ.

When I came out of the Castle a crowd of people had gathered on the Esplanade, probably to enjoy a twilight view of this ancient capital of Scotland. Edinburgh can indeed be proud of its beauty at this time of the day.

Suddenly I remembered that that morning I had been reading about the closes and wynds along the old Royal Mile, and I decided to make a tour of them. Only a few days before I had been taken by the kind, elderly Edinburgh citizen to see Riddle's Court and Lady Stair's Close, but I had no idea at that time that there were so many more. One book told me that even today nearly a hundred closes survive, each with tales to tell. Now I looked for them and I found them at every two or three doors. Many had only an entrance left and others had iron bars to keep visitors out.

I had not tried to remember their histories, not only because they were so numerous, but because each of them had connections with events outside my limited knowledge, so a mere name on the top of the gate of the close did not convey much to me. When I came upon the name 'Brodie's Close', however, I stopped short. The history of this one did seem to have left an imprint on my brain. William Brodie, the owner, had led a life of industry as 'Deacon-Convener of the Wrights', and of villainy as a daring burglar and murderer. I might not have taken much notice of Brodie had he not been referred to as 'Jekyll and Hyde' in one of the books I had read, and having recently seen an American film version of this famous story starring Spencer Tracy, I was acquainted with this curious personality. Spencer Tracy has always been my favourite film star, but since seeing his portrayal of Hyde I have been haunted by that horrible face, and have at last become reluctant to see Spencer Tracy in any other film, the emotional impact having been so great! Jekyll had been transformed into Hyde by the uncontrollable force of the medical compound he had evolved: how had Brodie conducted his double life?

One humorous story has been known to the Chinese for centuries. A certain man whimsically hung a Buddhist rosary round his cat's neck. When the mice discovered this, they congratulated each other, in the belief that the cat, their *auld enemy*, being now the proud possessor of a rosary, would in future be too busy saying his prayers to eat them. Overjoyed, they scuttled into the hall, where, without hesitation, the cat pounced, catching several of them. The rest ran back to their holes exclaiming in amazement that the pious appearance of the cat, far from having imbued him with charity of heart, was merely a cloak under which he prepared for action! I am afraid that many of us are two-faced in one way or another. The only difference between Brodie, or the cat, and the rest of us is the nature of the occasion and its results. Had Brodie not committed his crimes against individual lives and property he might not have been so notorious. I realised with chagrin that he had impressed himself on my mind more firmly than any other historical character along the Royal Mile. Is it not singular that the infamous Brodie should be remembered while better men are forgotten? And who will deny that Hitler will be longer remembered than many of those who have fought against him?

AN INCIDENT IN BYERS' CLOSE

The sight of Byers' Close reminded me of a comical tale I had read. In about the year 1757 there was a custom in Edinburgh for judges and advocates to don their wigs and gowns in their own houses and then, carrying their cocked hats, to proceed in state to Parliament House at the strike of St. Giles' bell at a quarter to nine. Most of these dignitaries then lived in the numerous closes and wynds, and while waiting for the sound of the bell they would lean out of their windows enjoying the morning air, even discussing the news of the day with some acquaintance on the opposite side of the alley. It is said that one morning two small girls, playing in one of the upper storeys in Byers' Close, were heartlessly swinging a kitten, suspended by a thick cord, out of their window. On the floor below lived Lord Coalstoun, who just at the moment when the kitten was on a level with his window popped out his head for his morning breather. The young ladies, in a panic, pulled the cord up immediately, but the angry little claws of the poor creature on its undignified ascent grasped the judge's wig, which disappeared as if by magic! Standing in Byers' Close I could clearly visualise the scene, though how anyone could imagine he was enjoying the morning air in this dark and narrow close was beyond me. I was particularly interested in Lord Coalstoun's *wig*, for when I was a schoolboy, some thirty-five years ago, I first saw a picture of an English nobleman wearing a wig. I wondered then at the amount of hair and curious hair styles of the English, which seemed to me as odd as does the hair of African natives or the long pigtail of our forefathers to the British. No one told me that the wig was an *artificial head of hair*. A friend of mine, Dr. Wang Ke-Chin, was recently called to the English bar and was photographed wearing a wig. When he showed me the photograph I could not resist laughing, for he seemed so altered that I scarcely recognised him. I am still amused that the symbol of justice is a *false* head!

I had been crossing the street from side to side in order not to miss the names of any of the closes and wynds, there being, fortunately, little traffic on the Royal Mile, which became quite deserted after five o'clock. It was perhaps the right time to see these closes and wynds in their right atmosphere. I zigzagged from one side to the other. The slope of the street is quite steep, and now and again I encountered an Edinburgh citizen with his body bent forward as if he had been climbing this hilly Street for years. It is a sight which I am sure modern transport will soon banish from Edinburgh.

AN EDINBURGH CITIZEN WITH HIS BODY BENT FORWARD

Hearing a curious noise coming from the opposite side of the road I looked across. An old guide was apparently relating the history of each close to a large group of Americans in uniform. He spoke into a megaphone hanging from a length of cord round his neck. When he finished talking he let it drop to his chest. He spoke very quickly and moved on before his audience could take in what he was saying. Now and again two or three members of the group would cease talking among themselves and run to overtake the others, and there was a good deal of laughing and chattering. It was an amusing scene. I must confess that so far this is the only guide with a megaphone I have seen in Britain!

A GUIDE AND A GROUP OF AMERICANS IN UNIFORM

A few minutes later my attention was drawn to a child of about four who was crying loudly outside the entrance to the turnpike stairs of one of the closes, while an elderly woman was shouting unintelligibly out of a small window high up the perpendicular column of the old round building. I assumed that the child wanted to climb the stairs to her home, and as there was nobody about—indeed, a lady who had just passed by did not even glance at the child—I offered to take her up. To my surprise she began to cry more loudly than before, and even refused to let me take her by the hand. I was comforted by the reflection that in China I would often see a baby crying at the sight of a foreign face, or a child shrinking away when an American or English missionary stretched out his gentle hand to make friends. Young children are apt to be shy of unfamiliar faces. I turned from the child and climbed a little way up the stairs. Everything was in semi-darkness, and the light showing through the little window at each turn of the stairs was almost negligible. Between the windows, where it was darkest, there was an air of mystery, and I could well imagine that in the old days of private feuds an assailant might with great advantage have lain in wait for his quarry in the darkness.

I was uneasy at not having been able to help the child, and wondered later how she had fared. Distressed though she was, however, she was certainly in far happier circumstances than thouands of Chinese children today. For those who do not know, China may be a country whose ancient civilisation and philosophy, literature and all forms of art are a source of admiration and wonder. And so they may well be: but how can it be denied that China is also a country of much squalor and poverty? I myself have had many dealings with Chinese children who had never seen a room in a house, and who existed day after day on a small bowl of cooked rice. When I held the office of a local governor I tried to remedy some of these deficiencies within my area, but I could not surmount the appalling difficulties. Since I

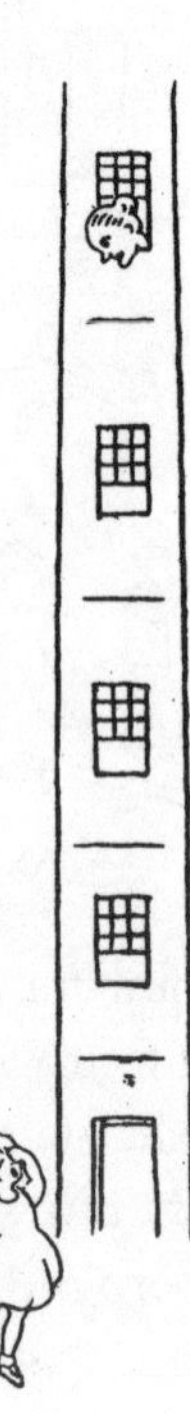

A CHILD OUTSIDE THE ENTRANCE OF A CLOSE

PRINCES STREET IN FOG

came to Britain, I have admired and envied the happy carefree lives of British children as compared with Chinese children. I do not deny that there are many happy children in my country, but their number is infinitesimal. The majority of Chinese parents are extremely poor, and I shall never forget the pathetic looks of their children. In my country, I am grieved to say, few wealthy or middle-class people give a thought to these homeless and foodless youngsters: are British people, I wonder, more considerate? How can we expect conformity of behaviour when the environment of the poor child differs so vastly from that of the rich child?

Prior to the International Conference on Children in 1940, at which I represented China, I had devoted much serious thought to the subject. I had intended to speak briefly, expressing my views on how the nations could help their children to enjoy and defend peace in the future, even if I had not sufficient time to describe the appalling conditions in which Chinese children had been living. When the time came, however, the long, excellent speeches of the other delegates left me feeling somewhat flat and with nothing to say; for the comparatively high standard of living conditions of British and American children was taken for granted, and any description of the poor living conditions of millions of Chinese children would have bored the audience to death. I was invited to sit on the committee which was to draft the 'Children's Charter'. From time to time I essayed a few words, but as the majority of the representatives were British and American, it seemed to me—perhaps erroneously—that few of them would care to waste their valuable time in considering the less fortunate children of China, India, Burma and other nations where standards of life are so much lower. Each item of the 'Children's Charter' was excellent and won my whole-hearted support and admiration, but I realised sadly that none could benefit Chinese children for a very long time to come. I am essentially a practical person, and finding the Conference useless from the Chinese point of view, I ceased to attend. The organiser thought me odd: I could imagine him saying to himself, 'How inscrutable *Chinamen* are!' After all, how many people spare more than a thought to those less fortunate than themselves?

My thoughts had wandered far from the little Edinburgh child, whose sobs had by now faded away. As I passed the Old Stamp Office Close, at 221 High Street, I could not help being reminded of the story of Countess Susanna, daughter of Sir Archibald Kennedy and third wife of Alexander, ninth Earl of Eglinton. She was one of the co-heiresses of David Leslie, Lord Newark, the Covenanting general, whom Cromwell defeated at Dunbar. With a face of bewitching loveliness and a brilliantly fair complexion, she had many admirers. But her fate was already fixed. George Robertson wrote the following account:

> While she was walking one day in her father's garden at Culzean, there alighted on her shoulder a hawk with his lordship's name (Earl of Eglinton) upon its bells, which was considered an infallible omen of her fate. Just at this time Lord Eglinton's second wife was sick unto death. When, therefore, Sir John Clerk made an offer for the hand of his daughter to Sir Archibald Kennedy, the latter consulted Lord Eglinton, as an old friend and neighbour, as to what he thought of the subject. Short and decisive—'Bide a wee, Sir Archy; my wife's unco sickly', said his Lordship, and the suit of the elegant baronet of Penicuik was declined. Two or three weeks later Lady Eglinton died, and within a few months the lovely Susanna Kennedy became Earl Alexander's third Countess (she was 40 years younger than the Earl).
>
> The old peer was exceedingly anxious for an heir, as his previous wives had borne him only daughters. Judge, then, of his chagrin when, in place of a son, to Susanna were born no fewer than seven daughters! He was so grieved at the lack of an heir that he threatened to divorce his lady. The Countess replied that he need not do that, for she would

> readily agree to a separation provided he would give back what he had received from her. His Lordship, supposing she alluded only to pecuniary matters, assured her she should have her fortune to the last penny. 'Na, na, my lord, that winna do; return me my youth and beauty, and dismiss me when ye please'. His Lordship was so tickled with this sally that he dropped the subject, and to his great delight before a year was out, his lady brought him a son, who re-established the mutual affection of his parents on a sure basis.
>
> In the Stamp Office Close she received all the literati of the time, among them Allan Ramsay, who dedicated to her his 'Gentle Shepherd'. Dr. Johnson and Boswell also visited her, and the former was delighted with his reception. The Countess died in 1780, aged 91, having preserved her stately mien and beautiful complexion to the last. 'The latter was a great secret,' it was written, but as it may be of service I divulge it in kindness to the sex. She never used paint, but washed her face periodically with sour milk.

There are many interesting points in this little story. Being a Chinese, I was particularly interested in the infallible omen. What a coincidence and what a fate! Many similar stories are linked with the marriages of well-known personalities in our past. Books on *China*, which I have read, mostly written by missionaries, and curiously enough one of the writers was a Scot, declare, citing examples of this kind, that the Chinese race is superstitious and full of fatalists. How true it is that one can see others more clearly than oneself! Again, I was interested in a divorce case being threatened owing to the lack of a son. Indeed, a boy is important in a Clan or Family system to carry on the name. Scotland of the old days did not differ much from China. But many Westerners despise the Chinese, who have been wrongly described as having no love for daughters. Though 'divorce' has never been set down in our ancient laws, a wife could be sent back to her own parents if she had borne no son to the family for a time. But human

THE CASTLE IN THE SUMMER HAZE

affairs became more complicated as time went on, and not every sonless wife could be sent back. So some clever Chinese, mostly Confucianists, devised means for taking another wife, even a third or fourth, while the others were still alive, on the excuse of wanting an heir. Very few girls, particularly with the wish of their parents, would like to become a second wife living in the same house with the first wife. Therefore came the concubine, who stood in a class of her own and who would not have fallen into that class if she could possibly have had another way of living. The curious part in a marriage life without an heir is that no husband blames himself instead of putting the blame on his wife. Oh, how many wives of my country have died of great grief for being wrongly blamed in the past! I wish they could have all stood up to demand the return of their youth and beauty from their husbands like Countess Susanna!

I did not enter John Knox's house to see its panelled rooms, its ornamental carvings and its pious mottoes. I did, however, peep through the small lattice windows which so resembled the windows of many old Chinese temples and other buildings, and the projecting gables and outer stairs interested me very much. In one of the books on Scotland I had read, there was a statement, hotly contested, that 'this venerable dwelling has no direct association with the life and work of the Scottish Reformer, whose residence, during at least the greater part of his stay in Edinburgh, was situated, as we have found, much nearer to the scene of his ministrations in the Church of St. Giles. It has been shown by Mr. Robert Miller, ex-Dean of Guild, and by other patient investigators of the town records, that the so-called "John Knox's House" was in these years in the possession and, for a period at all events, in the occupation of a goldsmith named James Mossman, a zealous Catholic and "Queen's man", who afterwards suffered on the scaffold along with Kirkaldy of Grange, for his attachment to the cause of Mary Stewart'.[1]

1 John Geddie, *Romantic Edinburgh.*

Though influenced neither one way nor the other, I read this statement with at any rate as much interest as I have read many arguments about the Shakespeare-Bacon controversy! Arguments by Chinese scholars about characters in the history of China would be even more abstruse, for many of our most famous men lived thousands of years ago!

The more I read about the hero of the Scottish Reformation, the more interested in him I become. Even before the Queen he was firm and undaunted. China, also, has had in her long history, and particularly during the early centuries, strong-willed, dauntless characters who, standing by their Confucian principles, defied an Emperor under the threat of death. They would have had little chance of escaping the death penalty had the Emperor been a merciless man, for they had no hope of impartial justice. Had John Knox been born in China under such conditions, it is fairly certain that he would not have acquired such fame as he did in Scotland. As it was, he was fortunate in having strong support from the mass of the people for religious reasons, and fortunate in that his Queen had not the absolute power of our ancient Emperors. Had China had an official leader of her state-religion, deriving his authority from the support of the people, her Emperors might not have been able to exercise their power so ruthlessly and the country would have evolved a democratic system of government and national life. Many of our ancient thinkers, such as Confucius and Lao-Tzu, framed the principles of democracy some three thousand years ago, but never succeeded in abolishing tyrannical rulers!

State religion can be of spiritual value to a nation, for it is a great unifying power. It is my own opinion that had Confucius set himself up as a religious leader, he might have been feared by the more evil elements in China. Confucius, however, was essentially a practical and reasonable man, whose ideal it was to convince by rational means and not by force. China is now so deeply rooted in Confucian principles that it is doubtful whether we could, even if we wished, adopt a state religion. The subject is complicated and abstruse, but I myself sincerely hope to see a strong, dauntless leader such as John Knox take his stand against the evil spirits in our midst, so that the uneducated masses may take their cue from him and learn to understand.

When at last I shook myself free of my thoughts, I saw that a group of children had gathered round me, puzzled to know what I was doing there, and I heard myself called a 'Chinee'. I turned to them. They laughed, and I laughed too. I felt that on the whole Edinburgh children were more friendly and easy-going than London youngsters, who tend to address foreigners by some curiously devised epithet. There has been much discussion recently about using English as an international language. Provided such words as Jerry, Froggy, Jap, Chink, could be dispensed with, that seems to me an admirable idea. I do not know whether other countries have similar slang terms, but I am sure that in China we do not describe people of other nations in this way. My own limited experience of the English language has instilled into me a sincere admiration for its dignity and distinction in the expression of everyday conversation. It is pleasanter, more diplomatic, and less hurtful to the listener's feelings than many of the harsh and rude expressions of the Chinese provincial dialects. I do not believe that in the use of these terms any superiority is intended, yet their very existence must necessarily be a drawback in the international use of this beautiful language. But who am I to tackle such a subject!

As I walked towards the Canongate, a group of children, making many strange noises and roaring with laughter, were enjoying themselves running and sliding down the slanting pavement. I can imagine that this has been one of Edinburgh's chief amusements for children for many years. I inspected the enormous figure at Morocco Land; had a look at Bible Land; and noticed the conical roof and projecting clock of the Canongate Tolbooth which stood out so prominently from their surroundings. I lingered awhile at White Horse Close and Canongate Parish Church, but in trying to recollect a few historical events connected with them my head grew more befogged than ever. In Canongate alone, occupying only a small quarter of the Royal Mile, there once lived, simultaneously, no fewer than two Dukes, sixteen Earls, two Countesses, seven Barons of the Realm, thirteen Baronets, four Commanders-in-Chief, seven Lords of Session, besides many other eminent men. Judging by the interest the British take in the Court Circular news in *The Times*, this fact must be of great interest to nearby residents! Considering how the British love the antique and traditional, I was surprised that this historic quarter had now so few inhabitants. Perhaps, after all, human nature seeks comfort first, and that is the reason why the city's population congregate in the New Town of Edinburgh. I wonder what the inventive American mind would make of the Royal Mile were it a part of New York or Washington!

THE CANONGATE

WHITE HORSE CLOSE

I glanced again casually at the projecting clock; I had not thought it was working, but its long, slender hands had met on six o'clock.

I had been wandering about for some time, and not only was I mentally exhaustcd, but my legs were trembling with fatigue. Without hesitating, I entered a small local public bar. It was not really a drink I fancied, but to buy a drink was to buy a seat on which to rest. There were only three customers, an elderly man and two elderly women, all of whom added greatly to the local colour. The man had a pipe in his mouth and was holding a mug of beer, while both the women wore black knitted woollen shawls round their shoulders, although it was August. Until my entrance the three of them had been talking and laughing with the old barman, but immediately I joined them they became silent and turned to look at me. I took my drink to a seat near a window, and they resumed their jokes and laughter. I confess I strained my ears to hear what they were joking about, but their brogue was unintelligible to me, so, instead, I interested myself in their gestures and manner of talking. The bar was very clean and cosy and drinks seemed plentiful. By the time I had drunk my solitary glass of beer and was beginning to feel giddy, a few more customers, smiling and cheerful, dropped in. It was a sobering thought that, however poor the homes of these people, however shabby their clothes, they nevertheless kept the many public houses along the Royal Mile—about twenty of them!—flourishing. An old story came into my mind. Once, a gentleman, living in an outlandish part of Scotland, talking to a very old lady, asked her if she had ever needed a doctor. She answered in the negative. 'What do you do if you are ill?' he asked. 'We tak' fwhusky' came the answer. 'But what if that does not cure you?' 'We jest tak' mair o't.' 'Yes; but if even that is not sufficient to cure—what then?' 'Faith'—the old lady began to be impatient—'if fwhusky doesna cure there's nae muckle use o' trying a doctor nor ony ither thing!' No wonder Scotch whisky is so renowned! The curious thing is that Edinburgh University has won world-wide fame for medical studies, and has produced many doctors! Perhaps they train their doctors to practise in other localities where there is no good fwhusky.

When I got up to go home I was completely intoxicated, not only mentally, but physically!

LADY STAIR'S CLOSE

vii
A Constant Precaution

'Another fine day for ye today.'

'Yes, and so it is for you', I answered the lady of the house. She smiled as she laid the table for breakfast.

It did not take me long to finish eating. I had no plan for the day, but Edinburgh drew me out of doors as usual. There was quite a crowd on the tramcar after it passed Tollcross, and the conductress was very busy with fares. A girl of nine or ten, two rows in front of me, surprisingly asserted that the conductress had given her too much change. It seemed that the girl had tendered a shilling for a twopenny fare and the conductress had returned her three sixpences and four pennies. When the matter was settled, the girl continued eating her apple as if nothing had happened. Some of the passengers smiled appreciatively. Mistakes of this kind must often happen, and there cannot have been anything very unusual about this one. But in wartime conditions it was pleasing to me, after what I had read about the spread of juvenile delinquency, to see such natural honesty in a young person. Almost every day I seem to see complaints of the increase of insincerity and dishonest conduct among adults, if not juveniles, attributed to the war. I have had a little experience of these cases from my four and a half years as a magistrate and district governor in my own country, and I can well imagine the difficulties. It is true that all over the world dishonesty inevitably increases when social conditions become abnormal as the result of war. I admire the well-regulated social life of the British communities; but as even among them ethical standards become relaxed under strain, how much more must this be so in the disordered and war-torn lands of China and the continent of Europe, where literally anything is possible! With these thoughts in the background of my mind I was deeply touched by the honest little girl in the Edinburgh tram.

In Confucian philosophy there have been two schools of thought: one holding that man is born good, the other that he is born bad. To the former, system and regulation exist for the purpose of preventing backsliding. To the latter, means and methods have to be found to turn man's natural depravity to good. The evidence afforded by the ease with which insincerity and dishonesty recur as soon as social conditions decline, seems to support the view of the second Confucian school. But the little girl in the tram swayed me to side with the former school. Had she not been naturally good, she could easily have kept the excess change, the value of which she would surely know. She might not have been able to define honesty, but she knew instinctively that it was not right for her to keep the extra change and apparently did not give a thought to the purposes to which she might have put the excess. Her mind was simple and her heart untroubled. We all, as children, have simple minds and pure hearts which, as desires multiply and the knowledge of good and evil darkens our souls, we lose. In the long history of civilisation countless moralists, ethical philosophers and wise administrators have tried to form codes of behaviour which would ensure goodness. Negative codes, all of them—systems of prohibition. The one essential is to preserve from destruction the simplicity of mind and purity of heart we possess in childhood. There is much talk about securing in the future freedom from want, freedom from squalor, freedom from idleness, freedom from ignorance and freedom from disease: all material freedoms. I think the spiritual side requires consideration also. The world peace can last if we are able to keep our minds simple and our hearts pure. A plan for *freedom from discontent* is needed; *freedom from too many desires.* It may be difficult to reduce desires, but at least let us not encourage the artificial creation of new ones. But this is a vast subject and I have already gone too far into it.

Getting down from the tramcar I mingled with the crowd along the north side of Princes Street. The many big shop-windows were not very different from those in London, and most of the shoppers and people on the pavements seemed to be English—when they were not Poles or Americans in uniform. I felt that this side of Princes Street did not belong to Edinburgh. It does not display the Scottish colours as much as Union Street, Aberdeen, which I visited some time ago, though there too the shop-windows resemble London ones. It is due to the ornament of the local inhabitants. Except this middle part of Princes Street, every other Street and road in Edinburgh is definitely Edinburgh's. Princes Street has, however, two very Scottish signs, one a shop with a big signboard bearing a long list of Scottish Clans and some such words as 'If your name is here we have your tartan', and the other a man at one end of Hanover Street shouting, 'White heather for luck. Lucky Scotch heather'.

LUCKY SCOTCH HEATHER

I explored the bookshops along Princes Street, buying a few books from one called 'The West End Bookshop'. The name reminded me of a little incident of the day before, when, on a bus from Granton, I heard passengers paying fares to 'West End'. I had not realised that there was a definite place called 'West End' in Edinburgh until the bus stopped not far from the Caledonian Hotel, and I at once concluded that the area round Waverley Station must be called 'East End'. So I jumped on a tramcar and asked for the 'East End'. But the conductress did not know what I meant, and in the end I agreed to her suggestion that I should go to the General Post Office. It interested me to know that there was no 'East End' in Edinburgh. Why not? Why should 'West End' be more agreeable than 'East End'? The questions are rhetorical, for during my many years' residence in Britain I have of course often noticed the difference in the faces between a person who had just been round Mayfair or New Bond Street and one who said that he had come from Pennyfield or Petticoat Lane. Most of my London friends loved telling me what good times they spent in the West End, but very few would reveal frankly, without whimsical or facetious comments, their experiences in the East End. I think the continuing existence of the social as well as geographical meanings to the names 'West End' and 'East End' in London is a black spot on British democracy. In Edinburgh, where there is no East End, at least there can be no invidious comparison.

Presently I crossed the road and had a look round the Greek Exhibition in the National Gallery of Scotland. There were many interesting objects in the show, but just think of three thousand years of culture exhibited in little more than one big room! Naturally it had attracted a good number of visitors. I was also interested in two watercolours by Girtin and one by Cotman shown in another room. I have tried to make a comparative study of British watercolours and watercolourists and have developed a great love for Girtin and

Cotman. These three pieces therefore made a special appeal to me, though I do not remember their titles. While I was gazing at one of them, an English landscape by Girtin, an elderly lady, smiling hard, put her head close to the picture. I thought that she must be an artist herself to exhibit such minute interest, but presently the nature of her curiosity was explained. Dragging a friend of similar age to the picture she commanded the title to be read out. 'They say this is Greece', she announced, 'but look, it is England!' And, firm in the conviction that she had caught the gallery Director in a childish mistake, she stumped off.

After an early lunch at the Balmoral Restaurant to avoid queueing, I proceeded to Calton Hill. Before the Register House I paused, as often before, to watch the local characters loafing and joking. At the entrance to Calton Hill I did not go up by my former route to the memorable guns but round the road of the outer ring just below Playfair Monument. It was a very fine summer afternoon. The sunshine was not strong but its light brightened everything within my sight. There was nobody about yet, for it was the normal time for lunch. Moving up the road I gazed about with a delightful feeling of leisure. At points I found a few tiny wild flowers, maybe dwarf thistles and harebells, among the grass. A small yellowish-white butterfly fluttered about, looking as if its wings had been heavily powdered so that it could not fly quickly. Perhaps, like me, it just wanted to linger round what it had found. A gentle breeze wafted the butterfly now and then. I would not have noticed the breeze but for the drowsy movements of grass, leaves and flowers. Then a slightly stronger gust stirred me to a quicker pace.

Presently I found myself standing on a point facing north-east. The vast expanse over the Firth of Forth made me draw a long breath and I felt an indescribable pressure on my eyelids. I found I could not open my eyes wider than half. It was the summer haze and the soft Scottish sun that created this soothing effect. Most of the dark-faced uninteresting houses immediately below were covered with haze, softening and beautifying their contours. How far the view extended I could not tell, for there seemed to be no edge to the sea, sea and sky being blended in one colour and veiled by the same haze. The nearer part of the sea was a very slightly greener blue than the sky. High above, the thin clouds must have been drifting though I could not see them move. In the distance a few slender white flecks indicated white horses on the sea, soundless from this distance. White dots of seagulls stood still in the air. Optically the whole scene appeared to be on one plane, instead of extended in distance and depth.

After some minutes of steadfast gazing I detected a small island, resembling a young girl's unplucked eyebrow, very soft and untouchable. It passed through my mind that I would look up the island in some book when I got home, but I rejected the thought as destroying its delightful mystery. I began to feel drowsy again. Certain half-forgotten mysterious words drifted into my consciousness from an ancient Chinese book, *Po-Wu-Chih*, supposed to have been written by Chang Hua (A.D. 230-300); and which describes three immortal islands, Peng-lai, Fang-Chang and Yin-Chow. They were called 'immortal' because their inhabitants were all immortals. Their buildings were of gold and silver and jade, their clothes of silk and brocade. Everything in them was lovely and beautiful, and nothing ugly or unpleasant. The inhabitants were free from hunger, want, birth, death, and all earthly worries and quarrels. For a thousand years or more since the appearance of that book those three immortal islands have been the Utopia of all Chinese intellectuals, and the name of Peng-lai, in particular, has appeared in many famous literary works, especially essays and poems. Were there really an island Peng-lai, who would not hope to go there? On the whole, however, we Chinese are not fond of the sea; our race originated in Central Asia, and we have remained essentially a land people. Very many of our forefathers never saw the sea! And perhaps it was for that reason that our most fanciful dreams were about the sea and places in it. And so, as soon as I saw the little island in the Firth of Forth, I asked myself at once whether this was not, for me at least, and at that moment, Peng-lai. Recalling my slight experiences of living on some of the Western islands, I preferred not to translate this mysteriously blessed island into a little land of common clay.

Another passage from a Chinese book, one called *San-Chi-Luch*, occurred to me. The 'First Emperor' of Ch'in (246-210 B.C.) once wanted to build a *Sun-bridge* across the sea to an island, so that he could walk over it and see where the sun rose from. To build a bridge across the sea *at all* in those days was fantastic, but this particular Emperor, though notorious in the eyes of our historians, is remarkable in being one of the very few Chinese who ever devised a great practical *plan*. The Great Wall of China, a thousand miles long, was actually built by this Emperor. Had he lived two thousand years later, the so-called *Sun-bridge* might have materialised! But I, though I *do* live two thousand years later, and though I too would have liked to walk over a bridge to the island before me—I am the last person to devise or carry through large material plans.

The sound of human footsteps quite near made me turn my head. A uniformed person was looking at me. We exchanged 'Good afternoon' greetings; he stood by me for a while and went on to speak of the fine weather. He told me that Inchkeith, the island which had started my reverie, was not often so clearly visible. He pointed out other notable places. Secretly priding myself on having detected his Scottish nationality from his accent, I asked if he was a native of Edinburgh or of some other part of Scotland. To my great surprise he answered that he hailed from Northumberland, though he had left it more than twenty years before. He was one of a family of twelve and had joined the army in the First

World War when only seventeen. After going through three and a half years in France and being wounded, he was sent back to Scotland to work on the home front, and he had stayed there ever since. He was now working at the Board of Control, York Buildings. His name was J. C. Lowe. Answering my comment on his Scottish accent, he lifted his eyebrows and said that one had to stay where one's wife and children were and make oneself agreeable to one's circle. I patted him on the shoulder and remarked, 'A very brave admission!' He laughed.

INCHKEITH

There was something in the day's paper about the situation in Italy, but I cannot remember how Mr. Lowe came to say that Mussolini would not die through *natural causes*. Knowing that Mr. Lowe was not an Aberdonian, nor even a Scot, I ventured to tell him a story which I had just read in a book. An Aberdonian spied a threepenny-bit in Piccadilly, stepped forward to retrieve it and was run over by a passing car. The coroner's verdict was '*Death through natural causes*'. He laughed again, louder than before, and we went on to revive other jokes about Aberdonians. I said that I had a great admiration for Aberdonian humour, and felt that we Chinese resembled them. I recalled a joke about a Chinese whose love of money was so well known that a rich man offered to give him a thousand *silvers* if he would allow himself to be beaten to death. The covetous one hesitated and then answered that he would let the rich man beat him half-dead for five hundred *silvers*!

Mr. Lowe and I were getting on very well. He said he thought there was time for him to go up to the Nelson Monument, so we set about the climb without delay. It was not easy, especially near the top, where one had to climb hundreds of very steep steps. Mr. Lowe went ahead of me and seemed quite untroubled by the steps; indeed, his ease suggested that of a sailor used to climbing the steep cord-ladders of ships and made me wonder whether the stair-steps inside this Nelson Monument were not constructed to test those who came to pay respect to Britain's number one naval hero: but knowledge of Mr. Lowe's experiences in France contradicted my thoughts. However, he revealed himself as a true Englishman by continually joking and laughing on the way up. I have found that only Englishmen show their greatest sense of humour in the most difficult moments of life. During the London blitz of 1940 I was struck by the number of people who joked more than usual while a raid was on. As for me, I helped myself along by repeating to myself the following famous poem by Wang Chih-Huan of the T'ang Dynasty:

> The white sun ends on the rim of the mountain range;
> The yellow river flows to the sea.
> If I want to widen my view to a thousand miles,
> I had better go up another storey.

白日依山盡黃河入海流欲窮千里目更上一層樓
右王之渙句

開襟俯城闕揮手拍雲煙
右駱賓王句

卻怪鳥飛平地上自驚人語半天中
右韋八元句

I wish I had been able to make use of this poem for Mr. Lowe.

When we emerged at last through a small door upon the parapet there were a young couple in naval uniform already there, courting and kissing. Mr. Lowe either did not see them or deliberately ignored them. Nor were the couple perturbed by our presence. But I who came years ago from the Confucian country where a young couple walking hand-in-hand in public is not possible, felt embarrassed at being so close to them and fixed my eyes upon the remotest distance. 'All the same,' I thought, 'what a place for courting!' I ought not to have been startled, for I have seen enough of such couples since I came to the West, but wartime lovers seemed to have more abandon and to be more dashing in their demand for affection than peacetime ones!

Lowe, knowing nothing of these thoughts, briskly pointed out the Castle, the Crown tower of St. Giles', the Scott Monument and the tower of the University Buildings. He tried to indicate where his place of work lay, York Buildings, but it was lost in the summer haze. We both felt the same satisfaction at being in this spot on such a fine day, and we drew a deep breath in unison. My mind harked back to my childhood when I once climbed to the top of the pagoda of Yin-Kiang Temple at Anking on the bank of the Yangtse River. In several respects the city of Anking, capital of Anhui Province, is not unlike Edinburgh, though on a smaller scale. My sensation on the pagoda was just like my feeling on the top of Nelson Monument, with the wide expanse of the Firth of Forth replacing the immense, winding Yangtse. Unfortunately not all the lines of the Water of Leith were visible to me owing to the tall buildings.

The following lines by two T'ang poets describing their feelings when on top of a pagoda could well be used to describe that on Nelson Monument. Lo Ping-Wang wrote:

I unbuttoned my coat to look down at the city buildings,
And waved my hand to pat the clouds and mists.

Chang Pa-Yuan wrote:

I wonder why the birds fly so close to the earth
It startles me to hear human conversation half-way to heaven.

Leaning side by side on the low wall we gazed around leisurely. Mr. Lowe showed me a scar on his right arm near the wrist where he had received a bullet-wound in the First World War. 'War does us no good', he said. 'My two sons are in this one. I wonder where they will choose to settle down if they come out of it?' 'Maybe China,' I remarked, 'as you have settled yourself in Scotland!' We exchanged wry smiles, each recalling his personal anxiety. I might have gone on to tell Mr. Lowe of the constant danger of extinction which threatened all the members of the big family to which I belong, but it was time for Mr. Lowe to go back to work, so we turned and began the descent.

We parted at the gate and I returned for another stroll by the National Monument, an unfinished replica of the Athenian Parthenon. Presently I sat down and opened the *Evening Dispatch* which I had bought in Princes Street after lunch. I found the following story: 'The story of the Calton Hill and the National Monument reminds a correspondent that about sixty years ago two friends of his who were students at the University, and who knew their Edinburgh well, often rambled on the Calton Hill. One day they hired an old guide and pretended they were in ignorance of Edinburgh and the National Monument. After much talk the old man, to impress them, held up his hand, and pointing to each finger in turn, said: "And this'll mind ye—Naetional pride, naetional ambition, naetional poverty, naetional disgrace, and the Naetional Monument."

It seems that Edinburgh is similar in configuration to Athens, and many Scots are proud to call their city 'the modern Athens' and to decorate their buildings and memorials in Grecian style. I know almost nothing of classical Athens and am, I admit, not qualified to comment upon this Scottish practice, but I cannot help asking why Edinburgh should be made to resemble Athens when it has a definite and distinctive character of its own. Why do Scottish people, despite their strong patriotism, wish to imitate other places? The answer must be the same as that which accounts for the existence of the term 'West End' in Edinburgh.

Edinburgh people, I had been told, are very cautious. Their shop-keepers will always say 'I'll *endeavour* to do so-and-so'. But this National Monument contradicted this reputation. Had those responsible for its erection been really cautious, they would have estimated the cost more exactly before actually starting to build. But perhaps failure to complete this monument was the origin of Edinburgh caution, and it now stands as a constant reminder of the necessity for caution.

However that may be, stories of Scottish caution are everywhere prevalent now; this one appeared in the *Weekly Scotsman* the other day: 'Two cronies met and were in conversation when a young man came up and asked the time. Wullie said he didn't know, and the young man walked off. "Why didn't you tell him?" asked Wullie's friend. "Because", said Wullie, "if I'd telt him we would have got speakin', an' he would have come alaung the road wi' us. We would pass my door. I would likely ha'e invited him in. He would ha'e met my dochter Jeannie. They would mebbe ha'e ta'en a fancy to yin anither. An' I dinna want a son-in-law that canna afford to buy a watch!"'

There is a similar story of a Chinese woman of many centuries ago. It tells of a man too poor to support himself from morning to evening, who picked up an egg one day. He went home and happily told his wife that he had found wealth. His wife asked when and how. He held up the egg and said, 'Here it is. But it will take ten years before my great wealth matures. If I take this egg', he went on, 'to be hatched by our neighbour's hen, I shall get one female chick when the egg is hatched. That female chick can lay eggs. We shall have fifteen chicks in a month. Within two years the chicks will have grown into hens and hatched new chicks, and so on until we have three hundred chickens, which I shall exchange for ten pieces of gold. With the ten pieces of gold I shall buy five cattle. The cattle will produce more cattle until we have one hundred and fifty head, which I shall sell for three hundred pieces of gold. The three hundred pieces of gold I shall lend on credit, and after another three years I shall have half a thousand pieces of gold. Of this I shall spend two-thirds on farm-land and a house, one-third on servants and a small-wife (concubine). Won't it be a happy day when we can both look forward to enjoying ourselves for the rest of our lives?' But the wife, when she heard that her husband intended to get a small-wife with his imaginary wealth, was furious and smashed the egg at once, crying, 'You shall not keep this trouble-making seed!' The incensed husband hit her and then took the matter to the local magistrate. 'This horrible woman has just destroyed all my wealth', he claimed. 'Please punish her.' The magistrate enquired what was the nature of this wealth which she had destroyed. The man recounted his plan until he came to the point where he would get a small-wife. On hearing this, the magistrate said, 'What great wealth it was, and all lost through the temper of this horrible woman! Certainly she should be punished'; and he ordered her to be thrashed. 'What my husband describes was not yet true wealth', protested the woman. 'Why should I be thrashed?' 'Your husband's taking a small-wife had also not yet actually occurred: why were you so jealous?' 'That is so, sir, but I thought I had better stop it ever happening', the woman answered. Surely a record of far-sighted caution.

THE WOMAN AND AN EGG

I, being a Chinese, am conscious of being over-cautious myself. It consoled me to see this National Monument in Edinburgh standing as a sign of the necessity for caution. I know nothing like it elsewhere in the world.

viii

Poetic Illusion

Though everything else seems to be growing, and even the length of human life is said to be increasing, life's span is still well within the limit of a hundred years. Alas, I have already spent nearly half my span: how, then, can I find time to study Scottish history?

What I do know is something about Mary Queen of Scots. Her romantic, tragic figure summoned me to the Palace of Holyroodhouse. Without her the Palace would be only a royal residence like many another, but she and Holyroodhouse gave me a poetic illusion.

IN THE COURTYARD OF HOLYROODHOUSE

ST ANTHONY'S CHAPEL AND ST MARGARET'S LOCH AFTER THE RAIN

In China not many old palaces are extant. Peking Palace, supposed to have been built in the fourteenth or fifteenth century, is considered new! But the poetry of the places remains. There are numberless famous poems by T'ang (618–906) and Sung (960–1276) poets describing the court scenes they knew and their feelings about the old palaces of the Han Emperor, Ho Ti (89–105), of the Six Dynasties period (220–588), of the Sui Emperor, Yang Ti (603–616) and the T'ang Emperor, Hsuan Tsung (712–756). I have no Chinese books at hand and I do not think I can relate any of these romances from memory, but the names of such palaces as Wei-Yang-Kung, Chin-Yang-Kung, Chang-Hsin-Kung, ChaoYang-Kung, Chang-Men-Kung, and Hua-Ching-Kung, though not a trace of them is left, have always fascinated our literary circles. The poets rarely indulge in description of the magnificence of palace life but rather show sympathy with the romances taking place within the walls. Most of the poems are in lyric form and their thoughts and sentiments evoke a sympathetic mood in the reader. Take, for instance, the following lines of Li P'o, inspired by the palace of King Kou-Chien of Yueh State in the warring states period (403–222 B.C.):

> Those court ladies were like flowers filling the Spring Palace;
> But now there are only partridges flying about.

Or these by Tu Fu:

> The thousand doors of the palace at the riverhead were locked,
> For whom did the slender willows and new rushes grow green?

Or these by Liu Yu-hsi:

> Because this is the place where the old palace of King Hsiang lies,
> Many girls of the present day still come here for slender waists.

Or these by Tsui Lu about Hua-Ching-Kung:

> Grass has covered the entrance and the tinkling state-
> carriage does not appear,
> The green-tiled roof of the palace in the thick mist of
> trees looks gloomy and cold;
> Solitary the bright moon rises and sails on alone,
> No one leans on the jade-white balustrade any more.

宮女如花滿春殿
至今惟有鷓鴣飛
右李白句

江頭宮殿鎖千門
細柳新蒲爲誰綠
右杜甫句

爲是襄王故宮地
至今猶自細腰多
右劉禹錫句

草遮回磴絕鳴鑾
雲樹深深碧殿寒
明月自來還自去
更無人倚玉欄干
右崔櫓華清宮詩

These few examples show the type of the poets' reactions. I am afraid my English renderings fall far short of conveying the beauty of the originals. The feeling aroused is intensified if the romantic events alluded to in the lines are known to the reader. Indeed, without those colourful romances it is doubtful if the palaces would have inspired the poets, and the names of Hua-Ching-Kung and the rest would long since have sunk into oblivion.

The poem by Tsui Lu well describes the feelings roused in me by Holyroodhouse, though common sense suggests that in the Scottish climate Mary is scarcely likely to have made a habit of pouring out her sorrow to the moon like a Chinese lady.

I have spent much time in fruitless wonderings about Mary. What would have happened to her if her first husband, the Dauphin of France, had lived to a great age and if their married life had been successful and happy? What would have become of Scotland? And of the relations between Scotland and England? Or if Lord Darnley had proved as capable a Consort as Prince Albert, what would this Queen of Scots then have done for her country? Suppose she had handled her romances with the skill of Queen Elizabeth? Or, on the other hand, if she had escaped the destiny of a queen, would she have become remarkable for her shining talents in languages, music and poetry, and would her beauty have secured her a happier romance?

Some of the criticisms I have read of Mary's foolishness and obstinacy seem to me unjust and even cruel. She was an infant queen, crowned at nine months: all her young days were spent in the sparkling gaiety of the French Court. She did not know the word 'sorrow' until she became a widow at seventeen. Saddened so tragically at this tender age, she received no understanding sympathy from her mother-in-law, Catherine de Medici. She was only eighteen when she returned to Scotland, further saddened by the death of her affectionate mother, Mary of Guise. What problems faced her! First her religious faith was put to the test by one of the strongest characters in Christian history. I have a great admiration for John Knox's character and sincerity, but I think he was ruthless in the pressure he brought to bear upon this young creature already so emotionally disturbed. Her Court was filled with intrigues to win her personal favour; she had no genuine friends, only men willing to sacrifice everything for her personally and without regard for the country's good.

The great test of a human being lies in his ability to resist temptation. Very few can resist beauty and the chance of power when these are linked together. So this radiantly beautiful young Queen of Scots, receiving lavish praise but no advice, had no steady guide and was encouraged to follow whatever path pleased her. It is not strange, therefore, that one calamity should have followed another until the final tragedy. Taking into account all her difficulties, are we justified in calling her foolish and obstinate? She has all my sympathy and admiration for restraining her temperament as much as she did. The romance of many an emperor or empress or beautiful talented favourite in China's ancient days ended tragically too. The fate of Mary Queen of Scots comes as no surprise to me, a Chinese. One of our commonest sayings is: 'Since ancient days the beautiful of face are usually unfortunate'.

Now let me relate my visit to Holyroodhouse. I followed a few other visitors into the rectangular hall. It is not big enough to make a startling impression (like the hall in Hampton Court, for instance) and it has no great variety of interesting detail—a few portraits of kings and queens, and some miscellaneous objects in cases on the tables. It may be that other things of historical and artistic value were taken away during the war; but my feeling would probably have been the same had there been many more exhibits. I did not stay to listen to the old uniformed keeper relating the stories of the portraits. I merely wondered why the painters had chosen such dark pigments for their work, making the hall still dimmer. The drizzling rain outside intensified the gloomy atmosphere. I moved to the other end of the hall and stood by a window. Though it was impossible for me to imagine the glorious Court receptions and banquets of old, I was sure to be right in thinking that this hall must have been lit by tall candles all day long; and while the etiquette, the costumes and the language may have been very different from those in our ancient Court scenes, there was probably no great difference between the outbursts of passion, cunning intrigues and fatal assaults which were witnessed by the walls of this hall and those that took place within the walls of Peking, now dim and empty too. Have these historical events, with their eternal consequences, taught us to mould life better in our time? Alas, one is forced to wonder whether human beings can learn by experience at all!

Presently I turned to look out of the window. The flowers and the trees of the royal garden and the wide open stretch of green leading to the majesty of Arthur's Seat offered a perfect view to the Palace dwellers. The view was the same: but in place of mighty kings and queens, princesses and nobles there stood to look upon it a humble being from China.

On leaving the hall I was struck by two small animal stone-carvings, one a group of pigs, the other a cow, which must have been used as door-stops. They were good and interesting pieces of work. Most of the visitors paid no attention to them, but to me they suggested two lines of a poem:

> Carefully I examine the little stone-
> carved animal door-stops,
> As if there were marks left on them
> by slender, jade-like fingers.

細認石刻欄門獸
似有纖纖玉指痕

Of course queens and princesses would not normally touch such things, but I liked to imagine that Mary might have done so on some occasion when she wanted to be absolutely alone. It was my fancy, anyhow. I did not want to finish my poem.

In the audience chamber I had a look at the two embroidered chairs. I knew this was the place where the Queen gave audience to John Knox, but I could not visualise the scene. Then we came to the room in which stood the royal bed with its decaying cover, curtains and canopy, full of the romance of long ago. I could not resist peeping underneath to see where the young French poet Chastelard lay hidden for hours, but I was only left wondering how he had managed to get into such a narrow space. The simple design of the pottery plates round the fireplace interested me, and I thought that they had probably come from Holland. I imagined those who had sat round this fireplace in every kind of mood, I also had a look at the tiny room where the Italian musician, Rizzio, met his unnatural end. All these rooms offered the visitor no splendours; their sole interest lies in the scenes they have witnessed.

TOPSY AND HER CUBS IN THE CORSTORPHINE ZOO

Holyrood Abbey, too, with its scattered stone coffins and tombstones of kings, nobles and bishops, seemed little different to my eye from the graveyard of many an old Scottish church or castle. A special case with a brass plate telling that the bones of many a king and queen lay inside announced most clearly the inevitable end of all human creatures. A poem written by our Sung poet, Lu Yu, expresses my feelings in this graveyard:

> The people of old lie buried on the bare hills,
> Their bygone traces can be found in tattered pages.
> Who knows the right and wrong concerning them?
> Lifting my wine-cup, I wish to ask the Heavens!

I did not discover who was represented by the two big marble statues before I went on into the royal garden. There were plenty of flowers in bloom, no doubt as bright and colourful as their sixteenth-century predecessors. A T'ang poet, Yuan Chen, had already described the scene:

> Dim and deserted is this ancient palace!
> The palace flowers display a dull, quiet red.
> But the white-haired court-girls are still there,
> Chattering idly about the Emperor Hsuan Tsung!

昔人葬葬荒邱裡陳
迹紛紛朽簡中畢竟
是非誰管得舉杯我
欲問盡空
右陸游雜賦絕句

寥落古行宮宮花寂
寞紅白頭宮女在閒
坐說玄宗
右唐元稹行宮詩

江雨霏霏江艸齊六
朝如夢鳥空啼無情
最是臺城柳依舊煙
籠十里堤
右韋莊金陵圖詩

But there were no white-haired court-girls left in Holyrood-house; only two white-moustached old palace keepers who enjoyed relating the romance of Mary to the visitors.

Before leaving I walked round the ruined and mutilated foundations and through tall grass to a group of trees. It was raining. As I stood by the low wall enclosing the palace ground some lines by another T'ang poet, Wei Chuang, occurred to me:

The rain falls over the river mistily and the rushes grow tall by the banks.
Six Dynasties have passed like a dream, leaving the birds crying pitifully.
Most heartless of all are those willows round the palace walls,
Still clad with clouds beside the mile-long bank!

What a poetic illusion I gained from my visit to Holyrood-house.

I composed eight short verses about the Queen after my visit, but I am not sure whether my rendering of them into English exactly conveys my feelings as expressed in Chinese. They are as follows:

I

The twittering swallows even flutter about in pairs;
But the wish of a beautiful angel is disregarded.
At the sounding of the guns through the heavy fog,
From door to door people are talking in surprise about the return of their Queen.

II

Glory and gaiety in palaces are what she had been accustomed to since her birth;
Her talents in literature and music are as flowing as water and her beauty as soft as cloud.
Other girls in the whole city avoid competing with her,
And the courtiers are busy surrounding her lovely skirt.

III

Five times the chief preacher has drawn her royal ear's attention;
The old Faith cannot be reconciled to the Reformed ideas.
Even her tears shed in her anger
Could scarcely move his faithful heart.

IV

Being afraid of listening to the bird's song outside the Palace,
Her heaven-born jade body too full of passion,
With endless song and feverish dance she sought to pass the long evenings;
While the poet underneath her bed lay there in vain!

V

The colourful phoenix without a mate was in search of a handsome bird;
How happy were all to know that the heavenly Queen was coming down to get married.
Who could foresee that the earthly bones were no suitable match for the angel;
In front of her courtiers she frowned all day long.

VI

The jade face, flushing red, displayed unusual charm;
With the candles burning brilliantly the whole night for drinking.
Within the Court ministerial robes and knights in armour, struggling for her favour,
Did not allow the musician to console her loneliness!

VII

The return of the brilliant state-carriage to the palace was only for a short while,
To attend a wedding ceremony in order to show her gracious affection.

What a pity her own husband died that night,
While her slender waist was still in the graceful dance.

VIII

Slightly painted with rouge as if to hide the marks of her tears,
Her tender heart was not understood by the audacious person.
Since the great ceremony of her third wedding, there were no happy days.
Hence the whole world condoles with this enchanting soul!

呢喃燕子尚雙飛絕豔天仙願卻違霹靂
數聲濃霧裡家家驚說女王歸
宮苑繁華夠習聞才情如水貌如雲滿城
佳麗爭回避怯煞公卿繞繡裙
主師文度叩天聰舊教新章難強同織使
嬌嗔和淚語忠腸不爲少通融
怕聽官前燕雀鳴天生麗質太多情酣歌
妙舞消長夜床底詩人空自橫
彩鳳無儔覓俊鸞天妃下嫁萬人歡那知
俗骨非仙偶竟日顰眉向百官
玉面飛紅別樣嬌高燒蠟柱醉通宵滿朝
文武爭承寵未許禁師慰寂寥
翠輦回宮祗暫離恩隆義重賀佳期可憐
夫婿陳屍夕正是纖腰縵舞時
脂粉輕勻隱淚痕狂夫未解說溫存三婚
大典無寧日從此人間悼麗魂

詠蘇格蘭瑪琍女王絕句八首

ix

Perfect Seclusion

Although it was raining when I got out of the tram at Church Hill, I decided not to postpone my walk to the Hermitage of Braid and, having made enquiries as to direction, I soon reached a big church built in red sandstone at the top of the hill. I would have liked to look over the church, but the rain was becoming heavier and my steps quickened involuntarily and I gave it only a passing glance, though even in that brief time I was struck by its warm, fresh look in the rain.

The rain by now was pouring down in such torrents that I could not see to the end of Morningside Road. From this point the road ascends for some distance. I did not know how far away the Hermitage was, and there was no one in sight of whom I could enquire. For a moment I was tempted to turn back and visit the Hermitage some other time, but the wanderlust was in me yet; and I could not possibly show myself less persevering than the Scots, so I walked on.

Presently I turned left and found a wide-open wooden gate leading into the front yard of a building backed by many trees. The gate bore no name, nor was there any notice saying 'Private', a common barrier in England. I entered, my last qualms of doubt dispersed by the recollection of a Scottish story I had recently read. The story tells that the late Sir John Forbes was so much annoyed by trespassers wandering about the grounds of Fintry House that he gave orders to his gatekeeper to stop them. One morning Sir John found himself face to face with one, Peter Sinclair, walking in the grounds. He signed to him to go back. 'Why, Sir John?' asked Peter. 'I have my reasons for going this way. I did not turn back for Bonaparte and all his army, and I'll not turn back for you, Sir John. Why, Sir John, I've been round the world and round the world, and have often been told to go forward, but never before to go back, and I'll not go back now, Sir John!' Sir John was given no chance of interrupting this spate of words, and after Sinclair had gone modified his order, telling his servants to 'allow no one to pass except that fellow Peter Sinclair whom the devil himself could not turn back!'

SIR JOHN FORBES AND PETER SINCLAIR

The Scots are as persistent when they believe they are in the right as the Chinese. We have in our country a popular story which illustrates how persevering we can be, though it concerns obstinacy, perhaps, rather than persistence. A father and his son were both of a pig-headed disposition. A guest being expected for dinner one day, the father sent his son into the town to buy meat.

The son, on his way home, when about to pass through a narrow lane, came face to face with another man also about to pass through. Neither would give way to the other. The father, anxious at the failure of his son to return, went in search of him, and on finding him at the lane realised at once what the trouble was. So he said to his son, 'You run back home with the meat and I'll take over this fellow'. Did not these Chinese possess the same spirit as Peter Sinclair? I have often heard say that there will always be Scots in the world: but will there not always be Chinese too? The Japanese invaders determined to conquer China in three months, yet the undaunted spirit of our people has kept China alive through many years of war, and will keep her alive for ever.

I walked on, following a footpath bordered by tall trees, and my feelings were soothed by the tranquil environment. Yet, as I paused to examine each detail of the scene, I realised that the tranquility was composed of sound. The quickly flowing burn, the torrential rain and stormy wind tearing through the branches and leaves, the occasional cry of a bird: each noise, distinct in itself, contributed to the harmony of the whole. This was tranquility such as I have felt only on a few occasions at a concert of Nature's orchestra, of which the wind, the rain, the tossing leaves, the shaking branches, the birds and the flowing water were the instruments. Somehow I felt I was not the sole audience. Hidden from my eyes, the frogs and insects in the grass, the fish in the burn and the moles and rabbits in the soil were surely listening. Some sheep in a nearby field had ceased to nibble and were lying with heads erect attentively listening, their little eyes half closed and their lips moving steadily. They were obviously an appreciative audience. They took no notice of me, a human animal with a head full of strange ideas, yet gradually I was influenced by their manifest contentment to take out my sandwiches and munch them slowly. The sheep had the advantage of me, however, for the rain could not penetrate their wool and they had not to eat their food out of a damp paper bag!

Presently sunshine came to brighten the field and a few of the more ambitious animals got up to nibble the grass. I too got up to go. A fine greenish vapour rose from the rain-freshened grass on the path as it twisted on before me. The only sound now that reached my ears was the clear, soothing gush of a small waterfall. I had reached an open space surrounded by tall trees and with a hill on one side. I could see not far away, built against the hillside, an old grey stone house. Along the foot of its walls were neat borders of flowers, and it was graced in front by a well-cut lawn, a fine layer of vapour hanging above it. No bird darted through the stillness, but a small chaffinch was hopping about near a tree, slowly, as if its feet were heavy. Presently I found on a stone a notice saying that this was the Hermitage of Braid, a gift to the National Trust from Mr. John McDougal, with whom, as I shall explain later, I was slightly acquainted. There was also a notice stating that the building was closed, but I would in any case have been chary of approaching nearer lest I disturb the peace. I remembered a famous poem by a very renowned hermit-poet, Tao Chien, of the fourth century:

Building a house within the world of men,
I hear no noise of carts and horses.
How can this be, you may ask?
A remote heart has transformed the place to solitude.
Picking chrysanthemums under the eastern hedge,
I leisurely gaze at the southern hills,
Whose colours, day and night, are superb.
The flying birds exchange social calls with me.

There is a real meaning to this:
I should like to explain it but have already forgotten it.

結廬在人境而無車
馬喧問君何能爾心
遠地自偏採菊東籬
下悠然見南山山氣
日夕佳飛鳥相與還
此中有真意欲辯已
忘言

右陶潛五古一首

細草緣蹊軟晴朝步
屧遲往來深樹裡啼
鳥不曾知

右明曾鐸散步詩

Even though here there were no chrysanthemums to be picked, the Braid Hills, and the unusual solitude of this hermitage within such easy reach of the town, made the poem most apt. Tao Chien lived close to my birthplace, and this seemed to provide a special link between Braid Hermitage and myself. Someone has since told me that this hermitage belonged to a Dutch knight who came to Scotland with King James I. He served the King well, and in return James built and gave him the hermitage. If this is true, then Tao Chien's poem was not very apt after all, for in those early days there must have been an almost continuous clatter of the horses and carriages of the King and his nobles coming to visit the knight. Nevertheless James I, the poet-king, may have seen the place with a poet's vision not unlike that of Tao Chien. Though time, distance and language might seem to create an insuperable barrier between the two, their love of solitude unites them. I myself was feeling perhaps the same sentiments as Tao Chien in his own hermitage at Kiukiang in the fourth century, and such sentiments are not confined to myself. Why do we dwell on our differences rather than our similarities?

HIGH STREET UNDER THE MOON ON A SUNDAY EVENING

I was filled with admiration for the public spirit of Mr. John McDougal, with whom I had had the pleasure of talking only two or three days previously, having met him at the other side of Blackford Hill. We did not exchange names during our conversation, and I only learned his afterwards by chance. He told me he had visited Iona three times, and his descriptions were interesting to me, for I had paid the island only one short visit from Oban six or seven years before and could not remember it well. When I said I was going from Edinburgh to spend ten days at Fort William Mr. McDougal remarked that Highlanders loved rain and talked about the weather being changeable if the sun came out. Having myself just visited the Hermitage in pouring rain—and it was even now starting to rain again—the remembrance of his comment amused me.

Presently I followed the twisting footpath past the Hermitage. The tall trees and hills on either side left only a small strip of sky to be seen. The Chinese poetic expression 'yi-hsien-tien', or 'a string of sky', barely applied, for the interlacing leafy top branches cut the string of sky into dots. The splash of a waterfall, artificially arranged along the Braid burn over a pile of stones to fall into a small pool, reached me, the sound of which was so deceptive that one could easily imagine it to be a natural waterfall among high mountains. It suggested a coolness such as we Chinese yearn for on our stifling summer days, but the Scottish summer can hardly be termed hot, and this waterfall seemed to make me shiver.

I walked on, and it seemed to me that I was back in my own country walking, perhaps in Hangchow, or Suchow, or Nanking, or along one of the many winding paths in the deep forests on the top of my beloved Lu mountain at Kiukiang. The trees on the hillside, with the Braid burn curling its way between, even the colour of the soil and the constant winding of the path, were familiar. I was brought back to actuality by the sight of a young girl in a brown raincoat sitting on a wooden seat eating sandwiches. The sudden nostalgia I had felt quickly vanished, for after a good many years' residence I no longer feel myself a foreigner in the British Isles. This country is my second homeland, with all its similarity in nature to my own country. The superficial human differences are unimportant; for, after all, are there not great differences between the peoples of northern and southern China?

THE FOOTPATH PAST THE HERMITAGE

Eventually I left the path and walked along close to the burn. I could hear the soft thud of my own footsteps on the wet grass above the occasional chirping of birds and the constant babble of gently running water. Suddenly a shower of raindrops pattered down on my head and I thought for a moment that the rain was becoming heavy again, but it was only a gust of wind which had tossed raindrops in a shower from the leaves and twigs. The wind passed by, and the leaves stirred gently for a while and at last became still. When, on lifting my head, I saw a yellow light on the topmost leaves, I knew the sun must be shining again. I recited to myself the following poem by Lu T'o of the Ming Dynasty (A.D. 1368–1643).

> The slender grass along the footpath is soft;
> In the fine morning my steps become slow.
> I walk to and fro in the wood;
> The singing birds are not aware of me.

I have always loved to watch flowing water. It has taught me many things, and in particular the aptness of the ancient Chinese philosophical comparison of it with the course of human life. The surface of Braid burn was as still and flat as a sheet of glass. Near the bed, stray weeds drifted by and passed out of sight. It must have flowed a long way, perhaps from high up in some hill, springing from a tiny source of raindrops, gathering force as it went, struggling ever onwards while waging a grim battle with impeding reeds, mud and stones. And what of my own life? I could not estimate how far I had travelled, nor recall in detail the difficulties I had overcome. What I did know was that, as the waters of the burn had at last become clear, so had the experiences of my life purged my soul.

Beginning to feel thirsty—no doubt as a result of the dry sandwiches and of walking beside the cool water—I was about to stoop to quench my thirst when I remembered an ancient story in an old Chinese book called *Nan-shih*. There was in a certain country a mountain stream known as 'Ku'ang-chuan', or 'Mad spring', so called because everyone who drank of it became mad. The king of the realm, to avoid this fate, had a deep well dug from which he took his drinking water. The result was that he was so unlike his people that they thought *him* mad. So they met to discuss means of curing him, and before long had experimented on the unfortunate man with all kinds of drugs and primitive surgical treatment. At last the king could bear no more, and in desperation drank from the 'Mad Spring', soon becoming as mad as his people. It was then triumphantly announced that the king was cured.

I thought with a chuckle of Mr. McDougal's Highland friends who, when the sun comes out, complain of the changeable weather. How man's thought is moulded by his environment! As I stooped down to drink, I reflected that I already had much in common with the Scots, and wondered if I should weld the links more securely by drinking from their burn. But what would my Oxford friends think of me then? I moved on.

A few stray raindrops showered down from the tree-tops. The burn babbled cheerfully. My eyes followed the flight of a small bird from stone to stone over the surface of the water. It was a pretty creature, with its white breast and black feathers, but its flight was not as swift, nor of as long a sweep, as a swallow's. It looked like a pied wagtail. The movements of the tail were fascinating: it moved up and down rapidly as though the bird's legs were bending and stretching. From stone to stone the bird bent and stretched, with a pleasant, soothing rhythm like the exquisite point-work of the most elegant of ballerinas, until at last it vanished among the bigger stones.

There is always something beautiful to see in the country, and it was not long before I espied a dragon-fly of dazzling blue, perched on the tip of a long blade of grass by the burnside. I have seen few blue dragon-flies, though I am told they are common in Britain. I was reminded of the brilliant deep blue eyes of the Highland children I had seen in Inverness-shire, which perhaps owed their colour (I had thought whimsically) to the blue of the Scottish sea in summer. The dragon-fly, poised majestically on his blade of grass, all four wings stretched

A DRAGON-FLY OF DAZZLING BLUE

upwards, made no movement save when he swayed with the grass in perfect harmony of motion. Suddenly he lifted his forelegs and passed them in front of his head and face, rubbing them together. Then he rubbed his hind-legs together in their turn, staring at me all the time with big eyes. It was as if a friendly Scotsman had, before opening a conversation with me, wiped his face with the palm of his right hand, rubbed his two hands together and said, 'How do you like it here?' I did not dare to speak aloud, but just whispered, 'How restful and quiet it is!' I could almost hear the dragon-fly's legs brushing against each other in reply.

By now I was near the end of the Hermitage footpath and could see the sun shining brilliantly beyond. Had I spent so long meditating by the burn, or was it just another quick change in the Scottish weather? Before going through the gate I turned left and climbed on to a rock by a tall pine tree to have a last look at the long winding path. From this end it held an air of mystery.

There is a Chinese story for every occasion. The Emperor Chien-Wen of Liang (A.D. 549–551) once said to his courtiers as they walked along the path in Hua-Lin-Yuan, 'One need not go far to find a place to commune with one's heart. Fine woodlands always make me think of the Hao and Pu rivers. I feel now that birds, animals and fish have come spontaneously to make friends with us.' The rivers Hao and Pu have symbolised a place of joy since our philosopher Chuang Tzu once said how happy he felt about the fish in the river. It was, of course, the Emperor's privilege to imagine that the birds, animals and fish had come to make friends with him. For myself I can only say that I came voluntarily to make friends with the inhabitants of the Hermitage for a short moment of my life. Oh, perfect seclusion!

QUEEN MARY GAZING AT THE SWALLOWS (AFTER A DRAWING IN THE BIBLIOTHÈQUE NATIONALE, PARIS)

X

Eccentric Expedition

It was raining hard outside my window; I could hear it clearly. But I had thought of going up Arthur's Seat to hear the Sunday morning chimes of Edinburgh's church bells. Rain has never prevented me from going out.

SALISBURY CRAGS FROM HOLYROODHOUSE

I might never have thought of this expedition had I not chanced to hear the chimes on a previous Sunday from Salisbury Crags. That had been a very fine morning, and as I sat on one of the public seats along the Crags I had become completely intoxicated by the still, yet fresh air. A shaft of sunlight hovered in the mist, suggesting the busy movement in the air of each tiny particle. Then the chiming began from one church after another. At first I could distinguish a single tune quivering through the mist with notes so clear and pure they seemed to cleanse my heart and shake old dusty thoughts out of my mind. Involuntarily I rose to my feet. More chimes floated up, each distinct and yet blending with the rest to produce an extraordinary harmony. I held my breath with a happy feeling of expansion and clarity until the peals ended in a soothing trail of sound. I realised how right our great philosophers and musicians were to say that music is best heard at a distance and from a high place. Perhaps I had been particularly fortunate in hearing the chimes washed by the morning mist. How much better this was than to listen indoors or in a street to tunes cramped by walls and tarnished with urban reek! I have read many tales of famous old Chinese musicians who liked to play their instruments in the depths of a grove or under the shade of a big tree in a far corner of a garden while the audience listened at a distance, or, when forced indoors, sat behind screens so that the audience could enjoy the music undisturbed. We modern people sit close together in packed auditoria watching the movements of the hands and the expressions on the faces of the players on the stage, and sometimes even daring—if it is winter-time in Britain!—to sneeze or cough.

The church bells of the Christian West sound much as our temple bells do, though the latter only strike single notes. They are cast in the same manner, and they are rung for similar purposes: the difference lies in their timbre. I do not know when the first church bells were cast in the West; in China there are temple bells among the ancient bronzes of the Chou Dynasty dating back three or four thousand years. We often use the phrase 'Sheng-chung-mu-ku', which means 'morning bell and evening drum', to describe something which awakens the mind and quickens the conscience, and it came to my lips as I stood listening to the chimes on Salisbury Crags.

I cannot resist referring here to the fate of one of the temple bells of Han-Shan-Tze in Suchow, which I saw some fifteen years ago. Whether or not it was the original bell cast when the temple was built in the sixth or seventh century I do not remember; like many Chinese temples, Han-Shan-Tze was rebuilt time and again on the same spot. The temple and bell I saw must anyhow have been of a good age. The particular bell to which I refer is known to Chinese children by its mention in a four-line poem by a famous T'ang poet, Chang Chi (about A.D. 756), which we learn by heart. Learned Japanese too have known the poem for centuries. It must have been one of the poems taken back to Japan by those Japanese princes and scholars who were sent to study in China in the early eighth century when the Japanese first thought of developing a culture. When the invaders entered the city of Suchow at the end of 1937 they arranged to broadcast the notes of this bell of Han-Shan-Tze to all Japan. By doing so they meant to tell their people of their military achievement in reaching Suchow. I wonder if the chimes reminded any of them where their culture had come from twelve or thirteen hundred years ago. It does not seem that their minds can have been enlightened or their consciences quickened by the sound. It is said that now this temple bell is in Japan. In 1942 I attended an International Art Conference in London at which it was decided to make a declaration demanding the safe return of all works of art stolen from their rightful owners during the war. So I hope to see this temple bell again in Han-Shan-Tze.

I am straying from my subject. The pleasure afforded me by the bells on Salisbury Crags led me astray. Before I left the Crags that morning I decided that it would be even better to listen to the chimes from Arthur's Seat. I could not go up there at once, so I left it for another Sunday. I prefer not to force myself to wander against inclination. Was I forcing myself now to go up Arthur's Seat in the torrential rain on a Sunday in Edinburgh? No, I had a strange whim to listen to the bells in this very different type of weather. Besides, I could be sure of being the only person listening on Arthur's Seat on such a morning. So came this Eccentric Expedition!

Before I set out in my hat and coat the lady of the house said to me, 'The weather does not look very nice for ye this morning'. I wanted to answer: 'Yee will not mind', but I suppressed the pun and merely said, 'It will probably clear'. I knew the route well and soon found myself walking along Queen's Drive towards Dunsappie Loch. I met no one. I could only see a little distance round me; the mist was so dense that it seemed almost to prevent the raindrops falling, or else it was that the raindrops mingled with the particles of mist. Only a short stretch of the low stone wall on one side along Queen's Drive was visible to me. It had no end and remained magically always the same length while I moved on. I must confess I should not have continued if I had not felt fairly sure of my way. One moment I was diving into the white foam of noiseless ocean waves, the next, I was being carried aloft into Heaven—until the well-paved motor-road undeceived me. Before reaching Dunsappie Loch I turned to the left and walked on the grassy slope of the hill, climbing steadily. Here and there a few yellow wild-flowers shook their heads gaily as if dancing to lead my feet. Now and then a chaffinch or other bird flew close to the grass to show me that I was not really alone. The rain slackened to a drizzle, then increased again to a torrent. The mist thinned and dispersed for a moment, so that the face of the hill and rocks was unveiled, only to be lost again a moment later. At times the wind blew hard behind me and I flew along; when it dropped I was lifted by the mist at every step. I was very hot, for the particles of mist clung to my body and warmed me with their friendship. A little poem formed itself in my mind.

The rain has no intention to
stop my walking;
I wave aside the floating
clouds at will.
On their tender stalks the
flowers dance voluntarily;
The birds fly very low,
maybe their wings are
heavy.
The green of the grass is
fresh as if newly washed;
And the face of the hill
becomes charming and
fuller.
My mood is for solitude and
remoteness,
So I climb up high and
await the sun!

雨無阻行意浮雲信手揮
莖嬌花自舞羽重鳥低飛
草色新如洗山容潤更肥
我志在幽遠臨高待日暉

雲雨中登獅子山 彝

Presently I reached the rocky part of the path and it became necessary to pick my way with care, for the irregularly formed rocks can be very slippery when wet. At length I found myself sitting on a small rock near a Direction-Indicator, and recognised it as the place where I had sat before. I closed my eyes, relaxed and drew a deep breath. It must have been still quite early.

For a while I thought of nothing, saw nothing and heard nothing, though I seemed to be still able to feel the activity of the mist particles. Suddenly one clear note, then two, very far away and not very loud, came to announce that Edinburgh's church bells had begun to chime. Not all the tunes could be distinguished, but when heard at all they were clearer and purer even than when I had heard them from Salisbury Crags. Oddly, they did not seem to rise to me from below. Modern scientists may or may not be able to offer an explanation, but to my fancy the bells chimed in the air above me, as if coming from Heaven. As usual, old Chinese legends came to my mind. It used to be said among us that one could sometimes hear heavenly music, played by immortals and the angels. Once a great general and statesman, Kuo Tsu-Yi, of T'ang Dynasty, before he became famous, heard such music, and when he lifted up his head he actually saw a group of angels playing all kinds of musical instruments in the clouds. Thereon he knelt down to pay his respect to the Heaven-dwellers. The chief angel or Goddess asked him what he wished. Before he could utter a word he was endowed with 'happiness, prosperity, longevity and many descendants'. The angels moved on and disappeared. But Kuo Tsu-Yi afterwards enjoyed all these four gifts. Now I was listening to heavenly music in a foreign land. Perhaps the mist was too thick for my eyes to penetrate, or the Western angels did not like the look of my flat face—whatever the reason, I saw no heavenly bodies, but I had sufficient happiness from hearing this music on Arthur's Seat. In such ineffable circumstances even a bird would not have dared to utter a note. Our great poet, Li P'o, once wrote two lines when he was on the top of a high mountain:

> I dare not speak loudly
> Lest I startle the Heaven-dwellers—

不敢高聲語
怕驚天上人
李白句

A most appropriate motto for me at this moment! In silence I composed a long poem of my own:

> There are many wonders in the capital of Scotland,
> But the lion hill is the first of all.

Though not higher than a thousand feet,
It is often hidden in the white clouds.
I come along with the wind and rain,
Climbing up to the top in the early morning.
I look on every side and find no boundaries;
Mysteriously it seems to merge with the gate of Heaven.
But how can I meet the Heaven-dwellers?
I sit down alone to enjoy myself.
I become relaxed and my dusty worries vanish;
While my heart is calm, I am able to be at peace.
Suddenly come the chimes of the morning church bells;
Sounding like an angelic orchestra.
They are far away yet near,
In subtle tunes of a thousand formations.
Where can I find the blue-bird messenger,
So that I can fly to and fro and linger with them?

蘇京多奇蹟其勝在獅山
雖不高千尺常隱白雲間
我來風雨俱破曉窮登攀
四望無涯際縹緲接天關
天人何可遇獨坐自開顏
悠然失塵累心靜始能閑
忽爾晨鐘響有如仙樂班
似遠復似近神韻千萬般
安得青鸞使飛翔共往還

晨登獅子山聞教堂鐘聲

Where?—I woke up and turned my head in all directions—where was the dog barking? I thought I was alone. But down below in the valley I at last espied a small brown dog barking at a group of sheep and chasing them about. He obviously wanted to have a game with them, but the sheep changed their position and resumed their nibbling. Then I saw that the whole scene round me had changed. I was back on earth again. When had the rain stopped? When had the mist dispersed? Had I been dropped from the clouds or had they risen higher in order to leave me alone? No, it was evident that I was no longer alone on Arthur's Seat. There was a young couple in naval uniform standing on the edge of the rock watching the Home Guard at shooting practice in the valley between Salisbury Crags and Boy Crag. The sound of the machine-guns stunned me. An old gentleman shook his head and began to climb down the hill. Some clamorous youngsters were making their way up the rocky part of the path, followed by a number of adults. I saw more people still behind them. In all directions, people. It was a complete contrast to the scene which I had been enjoying a moment before. Perhaps these multi-actions were already in existence and had only been hidden from me by the thick veil of mist. I had to admire the wonderful magic of Nature.

Suddenly a friendly voice fell on my ear. It came from the young naval officer who was accompanied by his 'bonnie lassie'. 'Well, what do you think of this?' he asked me, to open conversation.

'Very nice,' I said, 'a very nice spot here.'

For a minute or two there was silence.

'You must have been here for some time', he continued. 'I can see that your coat is wet.'

A lovable smile spread over his companion's face. She seemed amused at her young Commander who would not be silent.

'You know,' he remarked again, 'I have read some books by one of your fellow-countrymen. His views on our London and Lakeland are quite unusual. He sees things so differently from us that I find his books very interesting to read. But I have sometimes been puzzled by his illustrations. He does not paint the scenery and mountains as we see them...'

How small the British Isles are, I thought to myself with a chuckle. Then I asked him smilingly if he had any preconceptions in his mind concerning the Chinese. I added that many people living far away from China are apt to think, or have been told, that Chinese people have a different physical structure from their own—eyeballs oval or cubic, for instance?

'Oh, goodness no!' he roared with laughter.

'I don't think we actually see things differently,' I continued, 'but we see different things from the same vantage-point. For instance, you have come up Arthur's Seat. The first thing you do is to go to the Indicator or to unfold a map in order to identify different places. But we Chinese have such difficulty in remembering names of places and pronouncing them, that we have to gaze instead at other things which may seem too ordinary to you and may escape your notice.'

'Oh, dear me, by the way, do you know this author? His name is very difficult for me to pronounce.'

Aha, I thought, you are English and not Scottish. But at that moment the officer was called away by his companion to identify a place by the Indicator. I felt immensely relieved!

Presently the couple began to climb down. When they reached the stony part the young lady gave a small frightened scream, and her companion took her by the hand and led her carefully. I thought she could not be Scottish either, as she seemed so little used to walking on rocky hills, but maybe she just wanted to show off her stalwart escort! I was then on my way down too. Behind me came rushing an elderly lady who laughed heartily when she reached the lower part of the path. She kept calling 'Jane, quick', but her nine- or ten-year-old granddaughter seemed to have difficulty with the stony path, as did her white-moustached father, who was accompanied by a Polish soldier friend of theirs. 'She is a dear creature,' the old man murmured, 'but she is a little disobedient sometimes.' The grandmother stood further on, declaring laughingly that this was like *hame*. She must have been born in the Highlands. Was this not a revelation of the variety of human life?

DUNSAPPIE LOCH

Approaching Dunsappie Loch I saw a group of five horses being ridden up from below the gap between Dunsappie Rock and Crow Hill. They were soon standing in a line with their backs to the edgeless and endless sea-sky. It was a perfect silhouette. Later, as I sat on a public seat by the side of Dunsappie Loch, I saw to my amazement those same five horses struggling up the path towards Arthur's Seat. They were not going straight up, but bearing left. It was an unforgettable moment for me. No doubt those riders, three men and two women, were just out for morning exercise. But for the time being the whole environment seemed to belong to them, despite the multi-actions of the nibbling sheep, chasing dogs, jumping youngsters, rambling folk and practising Home Guards. I saw nothing but the movement of the horses, not even the lordly floating swans, nor the scandal-quacking ducks on the loch so close to me. How proud the riders must have felt! and how gentlemanly the horses looked! When they came to a standstill again in a line on the slope of Nether Hill or the Lion's Haunch it looked to me a wonderful picture with the loch in the foreground decorated with the swans and ducks. I have never been able to find a single phrase to express suitably my love and friendship for horses. Once for three years I owned two horses, and I remember the happy times I had riding up and down the hills of my own country. Now it is a good many years since I rode a horse.

ST. ANTHONY'S CHAPEL

The sunshine now gleamed on St. Anthony's Valley as brightly as if there had never been mist or rain. As I walked towards the ruins of St. Anthony's Chapel there were many people to be seen. A number of army cadets were streaming down through a sort of rocky hole on the edge of Whinny Hill. They looked most robust and active. While I sat on the doorstep of the ruined chapel they came and played hide-

and-seek among the ruins or jumped up and down on the heaps of broken stones; some of them made a slide down the slope by my side. It must have been a holiday for them.

For a good while I gazed on all these multi-actions of Edinburgh people, on the hill slopes, in the valley, by the side of Wolf Crag, near St. Margaret's Loch and along the Parade Ground near Holyroodhouse. Then, thinking of happy wanderings still ahead of me, I got up to go back. Passing the Palace and Muschet's Cairn I found myself in the passage where Younger's Brewery stands. I had already caught a whiff of malt before entering the passage, and although no drinker I felt I could do with a pint then. To my mind 'Younger' is a most suitable name to be associated with the making of beer. No wonder many a Scot prefers a glass of 'Younger' to other famous Scottish ales. But I had no real need of my glass of beer, for I already felt years younger by the wonders of this memorable Sunday morning! Was it not an Eccentric Expedition?

XI
A Fantastical Notion

The one hundred and seventeenth Exhibition of the Royal Scottish Academy dropped a fantastical notion into my mind. I call it so because it is only my fancy and because it will take a long time to determine whether this notion of mine can materialise at all. In the meantime it remains a fantastical notion!

Let me recall how it was born.

First I must say that I became acquainted with this Exhibition of the Royal Scottish Academy by accident. On the third day of my visit to Edinburgh I went round the shops in George Street, pottering in the old bookshops and looking also for some fishing tackle for a friend in Oxford. George Street is one of the finest streets I have ever seen. Its broad, straight length is lined on both sides with splendid buildings and at either end there is a beautiful square, one called Charlotte Square and the other St. Andrew Square. It has a stately atmosphere. Most visitors to Edinburgh will remember Princes Street first; but after walking there many times, I feel that its north side is a little too commercial and unstable for the name. It would have been a common street had it not been linked to the grandeur of the Castle. George Street, on the other hand, will always be magnificent on its own account.

After buying the fishing tackle and a few interesting second-hand books, I came out on St. Andrew Street and crossed over to the other side of Princes Street near Waverley Station. It began to rain heavily as I passed the Scott Monument. My newly acquired books were less willing to face the rain than I was, so I followed a large crowd of people up a few steps into a big building. And here it was that I discovered the Exhibition. This suited me perfectly and I at once bought a catalogue. To my surprise the seats were filled with people sitting close together quite contentedly, as if they had already seen a lot of the exhibits; but instinct told me that, like myself, many were only seeking shelter from the rain. An army officer's head was nodding jerkily in a corner. How conveniently the building of the Royal Scottish Academy is situated, I thought, and how thoughtful of the authorities to provide seats for tired people, as well as offering a feast of artistic beauty!

In the sculpture hall the first exhibit I noticed was a gilded bronze head of Robert Helpmann by Norman J. Forrest. It made a sentimental appeal to me, for I had only recently designed the scenery and costumes for Mr. Helpmann's ballet, *The Birds.* The sculptor had caught one aspect of Mr. Helpmann as a ballet dancer—in the role, I fancied, of 'The Wanderer'. I liked, too, Robert C. McNeill's 'Ben' *(Lignum Vitae);* H. S. Gamley's 'John Geddie, Esq.'; Benno Schotz's 'Sir James L. Caw', and W. Grant Stevenson's 'Stag in Bronze'. This last showed wonderful technique in blending the delicate treatment of the hair with the muscular strength of the animal. Miss Phyllis M. Bone's 'Crafty and Powerful' (a puma) and 'Good Companions' (three horses) revealed the remarkable ability of the same hand to depict two widely different characters. I seemed to have seen Mrs. Bingguely-Lejeune's 'Rudyard Kipling' in London, but could not remember when or where.

Among the oil-paintings, the pale colour-scheme and light brush-work of Sir George Pine's four works, 'Pigeon Hill Farm', 'Mare and Foal', 'City Horses' and 'Highland Terrier', made an outstanding contrast to the rest. Both James Cowie's 'Frieze' and Donald Moodie's 'Frosty Morning' were daring in their use of uncommon colours for their respective subjects. A. E. Borthwick's 'The Fugitive' appealed to me with something of Whistler's touch. The brush-work in 'More Snow in the Air' by the late R. B. Nisbet was very interesting and remarkable. George Houston had put a happy purplish colour into his 'East Wind and Daffodils', and Lieut. J. McIntosh Patrick could not have done a finer work than his 'Autumn at Kinnordy, Angus'. Besides these, I liked P. R. M. Mackie's 'The Hour of Curfew', John W. Manson's 'Evening, Whistlefield', A. R. Sturrock's 'The Valley of the Ale at Riddel', R. Payton Reid's 'Hark! the Lark', Frank P. Martin's 'Coruisk', Stanley Cursiter's 'The Island', J. Murray Thomson's 'The White Kids and Other Animals', J. G. Spence Smith's 'Pap o' Glencoe', Lieut. Charles E. Buist's 'March Morning, Holy Loch' and Charles Oppenheimer's 'Autumn in Galloway'. There was only one local scene, 'Edinburgh Castle', admirably done by W. Mervyn Glass. The atmosphere in 'The Herd Girl' with heather and cattle, by the late William Walls, struck me as most original and very Scottish.

At last I was in the water-colour room. Here I sat in contemplation for a good while. There were a number of exhibits which I liked: John Gray's 'Moorland Birches', Alexander P. Thomson's 'Sambo', Alastair A. K. Dallas's 'Dundurn Bridge, St. Fillans', Leslie G. Kinnear's 'Loch Garry', Kenneth J. Cuthbertson's 'The Vale of Portree, Skye', John M. Aiken's 'Castle Moill, Skye' and Mrs. Josephine Miller's 'Calton Hill in Snow'. But the late R. B. Nisbet's 'Landscape with Hail Cloud' and the late William Walls's 'Study of a Tiger' struck me more than the others. I also liked the drypoint of 'Dusk' by John Nicolson and the colour print of 'The Combat' by the late William Walls. There were fewer water-colours than oil-paintings, and they were less prominently exhibited. This phenomenon has always puzzled me at art shows in London too, since it is in water-colours that the British artist has always excelled.

It was a surprise to me to find some works by the late P. Wilson Steer, O.M., in this same show. A short time previously I had many happy moments going round a memorial exhibition of this great artist's work in the National Gallery in London. I was glad to have the opportunity of seeing more of his work, such as 'Dover Harbour', 'Portrait of the Artist's Mother', 'Landscape with Trees' and 'Walberswick Beach'. Nevertheless I felt that it was a little cruel both to Steer and to the other artists to exhibit his works on this occasion. No doubt the organisers had some reason for it.

During one month's stay in Edinburgh I visited this Exhibition about eight times, much oftener than I have ever been to any show in London. This was partly because I could easily get there to spend an hour or two, and partly because there were so many landscape paintings in the Exhibition, though still hardly as many as I should have expected to see considering the wonderful store of varied natural scenery in Scotland. Scottish artists should never lack subjects for their works. Judging from the deep love of all Scots for their hills, lochs, heathers, braes and burns, expressed so richly in their literature, the Scottish artist might well produce masterpieces of landscape. Perhaps I am too steeped in our veneration for landscape art. From my little knowledge of Western art as a whole I think the Western artist tends to concentrate on working out a vision to express the dramatic side of life, especially human life; the gorgeous display of human glory. Thus 'life study' becomes the main course for any artist-to-be in the West. The Scottish artist may not have been able to free himself from this training. I may be wrong in suggesting that in the West portrait and figure paintings find their admirers more easily than landscape.

But landscape art is the most characteristic type of our painting and the chief flower of Chinese civilisation. China, like Scotland, is so full of mountains and lakes and rivers that there is not one of us who does not know or love some of them. Our intellectuals have always had a deep affection for them. In the fifth century B.C. Confucius said: 'The wise take pleasure in lakes and rivers; the virtuous in mountains.' This may sound mysterious and fanciful, but it is easily explained. We think the unending, quietly flowing surface of river water can make us wise by giving us a sense of continuity and teaching us that new things are derived from old. When we look at a huge mountain we think of it as giving life to everything growing on it and being generous and kind to all living creatures inhabiting it. On the other hand, we realise how infinitesimal we humans are, resembling minute insects by comparison with the mountain. And so all egotistic ideas are removed from our mind and we believe that thereby we become virtuous. And as we all want to be wise and virtuous, we all love mountains and rivers. The Chinese term for landscape, Shan-Shui, means mountains and water, and thus differs in meaning from the Western term, landscape. That is why we esteem landscape painting so highly. Only in landscape, we are taught, can we enjoy depth and distance. Again: 'Nature is infinitely changeable and shows herself in different garments to different eyes. Every creation is necessarily tinged by its creator's outlook on life; there is no lack of variety in this main form of our artistic expression. A mountain rock, a few feet of flowing water, can inspire an almost unimaginable variety of pictures by different artists. A mountain ten thousand feet high and a river three thousand miles long may each be transferred to a square foot of paper: yet, looking at those scraps of paper, you remember what you saw in Nature and your heart and mind expand under the vision of her mightiness.'[1]

China is only a small portion of the earth. I have found the natural scenery of Scotland very similar to that of my

1 From *The Chinese Eye,* p. *75*

own country. Perhaps this is why Chinese and Scots have so much in common in their human nature. Among many British masters, I have always enjoyed intensely looking at the works of Sir D. Y. Cameron, R.A., especially his pen-and-ink wash drawings. Unfortunately there was none of his work in this Exhibition.

As I have mentioned before, in beauty and artistic representation there is no difference between West and East. Our works differ from each other only in technique and medium; and these differences are ones which exist between *any* two artists, whether they be of the West or the East. But such differences cannot debar the Easterner from admiring a great Western work of art, or vice versa. Moreover, I have noticed that the British and the Chinese are both very fond of one medium of art, the watercolour. Britain has a good water-colour tradition, to quote the late Laurence Binyon. The British prefer *transparent* water-colours to the body-colours which are used on the European Continent. Britain has produced in the past many great water-colourists such as Paul Sandby, Alexander and J. R. Cozens, Francis Towne, Rowlandson, Blake, Girtin, Turner, Cotman, Constable, De Wint and Cox. We Chinese have been practising water-colours for about two thousand years, and water-colour is the only medium for our pictorial art. It is a point in common between our two countries. The great Exhibition of Chinese Art at Burlington House in 1935–36 proved the enthusiasm and admiration for Chinese works of art among all Britishers.

Art is an international language which, unlike a spoken language, can be understood by all peoples. The Second World War has made everything chaotic and difficult, but I think it has at the same time brought all of us peace-loving peoples closer together, and it is natural that we should try to understand each other better than before. What better way could there be than through the international language of art? Tolstoy said that the task of art is enormous. 'Through

LADY STAIR'S HOUSE

the influence of real art, aided by science, guided by religion, that peaceful co-operation of man which is now maintained by external means—by our law courts, police, charitable institutions, factory inspections and so forth—should be obtained by man's free and joyous activity. Art should cause violence to be set aside!' Now is the time for us, especially artists, art lovers and art critics, to carry out this enormous task. Art represents the mind and life of the people that creates it, and at the same time has a universal appeal to man's passion for beauty. After this Second World War I sincerely hope that there will be an International Art Body set up with the responsibility of arranging frequent interchanges of works of art, on exhibition, as well as of all types of handicrafts. China would appreciate tremendously such a scheme, for she probably owns fewer examples of foreign art than any other country, and it would be well-nigh impossible for her, especially in view of her currency problems, to acquire at this date a permanent store of foreign masterpieces.

The establishment of this International Art Body is my fantastical notion. I admit that there are in existence such bodies as an International Artists' Association and the like, but they are working for different aims from mine. In fact, those international organisations for art can hardly be called 'international' because their centre is invariably in Paris or London and their membership is inevitably limited to nationals of European countries, neither America nor Russia being represented, not to mention the Middle and Far East. I would like to see this International Art Body running on similar lines to the International P.E.N. Club and the Olympic Games. I think it could make a practical contribution to the maintenance of world peace. It should include all art lovers, and critics as well as artists. (I should prefer that artists should not take an active part in its administration, lest we let personal feelings sway our judgment.) The Body should have a centre in the capital of every nation of the world, where exhibitions and lectures could be held. The central Body would need to seek the support of the different Governments, so that loans of valuable masterpieces could be arranged under suitable safeguards. It should also arrange exchanges of art professors and art critics and also of craftsmen to explain techniques. An organisation for world food distribution has been formed: why not an organisation for world mental food distribution too?

As the first step towards this International Art Body I would suggest the launching of an *International Art Fund*, quite independent of the political issues dividing nations. Surely many artists would be willing to contribute one outstanding work for a beginning!

In the catalogue of the hundred and seventeenth Exhibition of the Royal Scottish Academy I read about the 'Guthrie Award': the President and Committee for the year would award a prize— the interest on one thousand pounds— to the best work shown at the Exhibition by a young Scottish artist. The work selected might be from any of the three branches of art represented in the Academy, and would be decorated by a shield specially designed for the purpose. This makes me feel sure that there are many more art lovers who would support my I.A.B. My fantastical notion may take a long time to materialise. If it does materialise I shall always feel grateful to the hundred and seventeenth Exhibition of the Royal Scottish Academy.

REID'S CLOSE

xii
Nostalgic Sensation

One morning in early May 1944 I lay wide awake in bed in a small Edinburgh hotel turning the pages of a little volume of Shakespeare. I do not always understand Shakespeare but these lines were easy:

> When daisies pied, and violets blue,
> And lady-smocks all silver-white,
> And cuckoo-buds of yellow hue,
> Do paint the meadows with delight:
> The cuckoo then on every tree
> Sings, CuckOO-cuckOO.

This recalled to my mind the lines of Robert Burns:

> Common friends to you and me,
> Nature's gifts to all are free.

Why was I in bed? I jumped up and prepared to go out immediately, but was at first uncertain where to go. I wanted a change from my other expeditions. Places of historical interest did not suit my mood, and I finally decided to wander round the Royal Botanic Garden, which I had visited before.

The Botanic Garden is well situated and very easy to reach from the centre of the city. The rain stopped as I went out and took a tramcar to Hanover Street and then another to the Garden. Remembering my favourite haunts, I first went to the Rock Garden, where masses of different heathers were about to open their tiny buds. I had seen this glorious purple carpet a year before and had been amazed at the variety of species, a number of which come from America. As Scotsmen always take great pride in their heathers, it is fitting that there should be a good show of them in their Botanic Garden. What they regard as the true heather is called Ling and has cross-leaves up the stalk and a cluster of big bell-like flowers at the top. I do not remember anything particular about the heathers in my own country. We have a herbal plant, the name of which, phonetically, is Ling, though it is not a heather. It is curious that two countries as far apart as China and Scotland have the same word for a native plant although Chinese is a monosyllabic language and English a polysyllabic. Ling sounds to me more like a Chinese word than an English one, and I wondered how it came to be used for a species of heather. Perhaps botanists can explain it, or maybe there is a local legend about it.

Heather, I am told, is the best flower for honey. Not only can the bees easily penetrate the bell-like flowers but heather honey has a particularly rich colour and flavour. Scotland, with its abundance of heather, produces large quantities of good honey; and my other books have been the means of earning me delightful presents of honey from Scottish friends.

Presently I came to another favourite haunt, the small lake or pool. I stood on the brink looking towards a group of pine trees slightly to my right, whose strong blackish trunks and twisted branches with their masses of deep blue needles commanded the scene. In front of the pines many trees of varying heights and shades of green formed a sort of slope, their long, slender branches, some adorned with small flowers, hanging right down into the water. A small punt floated near by. Close to where I stood was a large cluster of water-lily leaves and buds; otherwise the smooth surface of the water was only broken by a few reeds sticking up here and there. As there was no wind, I could detect one or two blue dragon-flies clinging to the top of the reeds. On my left was a low rhododendron bush in full bloom, covered with clusters of five or six brilliant vermilion flowers. Many fine species of rhododendrons have comc from my country, and they are linked in my mind with China just as heather is with Scotland. It is always a joy to me to see them in bloom. This vermilion variety lent just the right touch to the surrounding colour scheme. A little way beyond this rhododendron, but still at the water's edge, was a tall tree with emerald-green leaves, and next to it another one whose yellowish-green leaves were just coming out. Most attractive of all was a weeping willow with all its slender yellow branches drooping round it like silken tassels. Beneath such a delectable umbrella, who but a queen could be seated? Round the foot of the willow and a little way along the water's edge grew huge rhubarb-like leaves which added a decorative note to the scene and broke the monotony of the small leaves of the trees. The scene was harmonious in every detail. Not a single leaf was stirring except to breathe gently after the refreshing rain. When they all breathed together, a thin mist or vapour formed over the lake. My clothes felt saturated with moisture.

Two small birds fluttered round the willow, quite undisturbed by the rapid approach of a pair of ducks, one with shiny green feathers round the head and the other with brown and black spotted plumage, who came skimming over the surface of the lake and then continued on their way floating side by side, occasionally turning in small circles. They were quacking softly as though whispering to each other how peaceful it was there. I searched my pocket and threw them the few crumbs I found there. At first they showed signs of acknowledging my advances, but perhaps they were only startled by my movement for they then went on their way without a single peck at the crumbs. I threw them some more and they still paid no heed. I could not understand why my offering should be received so coldly, since they could not already be full of crumbs so early in the morning. However, I thought that they might need the crumbs later on, so I threw all I had into the water. To my surprise the ducks at once took to the wing and flew towards the willow tree, landing on the water near the rhubarb leaves. I was greatly intrigued by their picturesque flight and by the way they skimmed over the surface. I wanted to watch them further, so I walked slowly towards the rhubarb leaves, but as I approached a big tree still rather bare of leaves the ducks must have noticed me for they flew off again at once in the direction from which they had come and landed on the little punt. After a minute they disappeared into the thick foliage behind. I was rather piqued at their unfriendly attitude, but gradually I realised that I must have misunderstood them. For they were surely in love and had no need of food or attention from others. I had acted selfishly in trying to attract their attention and no doubt they had whispered to each other, 'How silly men are. This one just won't let us alone!' I thought it was time I moved on. A little poem came into my mind:

Spring water crystallises all
the new greens
Spring heart is floating on
the water.
The gentle pair of lovely
ducks
Also know love-making.

春水凝新碧
春心水上浮
輕盈雙瑞鴨
也解說温柔
池鴨吟

I examined the label on the tree near me, and it read 'Oriental Plane' or 'Platanus Orientalis, Orient'. I could not claim that this particular specimen had come from China, but I am sure that there are many of these trees in my country. Its young leaves looked like those of the sycamore or of what the Americans call the buttonwood tree. It was somewhat similar to the Chinese tree *Wutung*, from the seeds of which is extracted the famous Chinese wood oil. The *Wutung* has inspired many of our men of letters and I could recite many poems about it.

Spring had certainly come to the Royal Botanic Garden. On my side of the lake I saw many flowering trees and shrubs, somc almond and apple trees, and a great many rhododendrons of different colours. These were scattered among the big trees, and their vivid red colouring showed up well against the fresh yellowish-green of the trees and the darker green of the grass. The sight made me feel so cheerful that I wanted to dance instead of walking slowly. However, the stately pines with their deep-blue needles seemed to counsel me to adopt a more dignified gait.

THE STATELY PINES

A few blackbirds and robins were hard at work pecking for worms, but without much success. Remembering my experience with the ducks on the lake, I did not stop to watch them. I noticed a pair of chaffinches flying from one rhododendron bush to another, finally vanishing into a clump of trees. I heard so many birds singing that it sounded like a contest.

Presently I passed an old house set among the trees and bushes, in which I supposed the keeper of the Garden to live. I did not go in, for I knew nobody and did not want to ask any botanical questions as I had done on one or two occasions before. The house was built on the top of a small mound, the slopes of which stretched out all round it like a wide Elizabethan skirt of bright green velvet, studded here and there with rhododendrons. I went round to the back of the building and then down the slope so quickly that I felt as though I were sliding, a sensation which was increased by the smoothness of the green grass. Then I slid down another mound and yet a third. The whole surface of this Garden is undulating, which I find very pleasing.

I noticed a spot which looked much brighter than anything I had seen hitherto, rather like a charcoal fire throwing sparks through the dark tree trunks. Occasionally a shaft of sunlight shone on it. I hastened towards it and saw there were masses of rhododendrons and azaleas in full bloom. They evidently thrive in Scottish soil. I remembered that there is a rhododendron house in this Garden, but the thought of it did not tempt me to leave this spectacular outdoor show. From a distance there appeared to be a very thin layer of coloured mist covering all the blooms and I would not go too close for fear of spoiling the magical effect. The Chinese call such a mist 'Hwa-wu' or 'Flowery mist'. A single bloom on a slender stalk with a few leaves perfectly attached needs to be looked at very closely if its beauty is to be fully appreciated. But when masses of flowers are seen blooming together amid abundant dark green foliage one should half-close one's eyes, as I did now, to get the best effect of the rich colour.

In the Garden I also saw a few magnolia trees in bloom and one or two wisterias about to flower.

I thought at first that I had never seen such a glorious display of rhododendrons anywhere before. But then I remembered that I had, though the circumstances were very different. Just after I relinquished my post as governor and magistrate of my home district, Kiukiang, I was having a holiday in a small house near Ta-ling-chung high up on Lu mountain. It was in April or May and still very cold at that height and there were not yet many visitors. I met, however, one young lady whom I knew and we decided to make a day's expedition to Black-Dragon Pool, a natural lake at the foot of a great waterfall. Lu mountain is renowned for rocky scenery and waterfalls, and they have been sung and painted by our great poets and artists ever since the fourth century. Of the many beautiful natural pools scattered over the mountain-side, the three called Black-Dragon Pool, White-Dragon Pool and Yellow-Dragon Pool are the finest, and to my mind Black-Dragon Pool with its wonderful surroundings is the finest of all. My friend set out with a basket of food, which I carried. This small burden was itself a pleasant novelty to me after the excessive attention of servants in the district governorship. Avoiding Kuling High Street, already more than two thousand feet above sea-level, we took a footpath upward. At a few rocky points we had to crawl, but were involved in no serious climbing. Over most of the route, the footpath is good, part of it is even paved with stones, since it is a normal road of travellers going from the north side of the mountain to the south. Kiukiang District lies to the north, the capital city being close to the Yangtse River. To the south is the District of Hsin-Tzu, from whence people can travel to other places by way of the great Poyang Lake, one of the five largest in China, or by crossing Lu mountain to Kiukiang and hence along the Yangtse. The footpath is very ancient. In summer travellers from both sides of the mountain like to travel by it in order to enjoy the beautiful scenery. Some people do the journey one side to the other in a single day. Others take two days and stay the night in one of the little inns or hotels at Kuling. We did not keep strictly to the footpath, but went our own way at a pace, occasionally stopping to rest. We did not talk much, having nothing particular to say. Birds flew past us chattering loudly; flowers seemed to give us inquiring glances as we passed. We did not slacken our pace until, going down a slope not far from our destination, we suddenly stopped to stare in delighted amazment at the large slope packed with wild rhododendrons and azaleas in full bloom, a mass of red, pink and yellow. Eventually my friend moved, but instead of going forward, went back to find a rock higher up to sit on. I followed her and we sat down with two tall, crooked pine trees at our backs. The broad pine branches sheltered us from a sudden shower which fell a few minutes later, and we sat there watching the flowers take their bath and then exude a coloured mist. As it was not raining hard, each flower seemed to welcome it, some of them even twisting their heads a little to catch their share. When the rain stopped we continued to sit there oblivious of time. My friend composed a short verse and I did the same. When we recited our compositions to each other, we found them more or less the same in thought though different in wording. Eventually we turned home without ever reaching Black-Dragon Pool. And I even forgot the basket. That happy day came back to me as I gazed at these rhododendrons and azaleas in Edinburgh!

Once upon a time I used to write love poems, in which flowers invariably figured as a background. The following five short poems concern five different flowers: yulan or white magnolia, camelia, azalea, wisteria and rhododendron. All except the first named were in this Garden.

JEALOUSY

A tree full of jade and gems deserves a careful look;
But my heart is full of bitter jealousy.
I ask my love to roll up my silken sleeves.
'How do my arms compare with the yulan?'

TENDERNESS

My spring robe reveals my slender figure.
I stand at the window smoothing back my hair.
My love puts into my hair a red camelia.
I smile to him and wonder if he has been standing there behind me all the time.

LOVE

My love looks flushed with wine and smilingly mocks at my blushing face,
While we go hand in hand in search of the colourful spring.
It is not the azaleas which are on fire,
But love that has made our hearts to burn!

WAITING

Gently the breeze blows on the thin silk skirt.
A jade-like figure bends forward, knitting her willow-leaf brows.
She holds a bundle of tangled love knots,
And, angrily glancing, slowly counts the blooms of the wisteria.

SPRING

In a light gown softly I come to the garden;
A knot of loving thoughts lies locked within my heart.
I steal round to the rhododendron bush.
The colour of the flowers and of my face will be difficult for my love to distinguish.

一樹瓊瑤着意看酸心未許怯春寒情郎挽起雙羅袖儂腕伸如白玉蘭

春衫襯出好腰肢斜倚窗前理鬢絲插上山茶紅一朶笑郎背立可多時

阿郎如醉哂儂嬌攜手尋春春色饒不是杜鵑花似火祇緣情愛兩心燒

習習輕風薄薄紗柳眉不展玉身斜一束情絲千萬曲含嗔細數紫藤花

輕裝淺步入園來一脈情思撒不開偷向石楠花後立花容人面費郎猜

情詩絕句五首

In Chinese symbolism we identify girls with flowers. At one time I wanted to write a book of short poems like those quoted above, covering all the popular flowers of my country, but I have never achieved it, for there are far too many flowers in China and one cannot summon the appropriate mood at will.

Most of the flowers which now flourish in every garden in the British Isles were originally imported into the country, and many of them were brought from China, often only after much trouble on the part of collectors. I believe that the Edinburgh Royal Botanic Garden has had close connections with flower-hunting in China. For instance, the well-known George Forrest of Falkirk, after working in the Royal Botanic Garden for some time, was sent on several expeditions to China to collect plants and he brought back many new ones with him. This may explain why the Royal Botanic Garden has such a glorious show of rhododendrons and azaleas. Forrest spent most of his time in Yunnan Province and did not visit my homeland, Kiukiang. Charles Manes is one of the very few collectors who have been up Lu mountain. I am no botanist and know very little about flower distribution in China, but I do know that the flora of Hupeh is considered to be specially rich and the Province has in consequence been visited by many Western collectors. Kiukiang is very close to Hupeh, and perhaps it was thought that plants which grew on Lu mountain must have already been collected in Hupeh. For my part I doubt if this is so, and I hope the day will come when I shall see a plant from Kiukiang decorating the gardens of the world! I must admit that in some cases, with the help of scientific study and methods, rhododendrons and azaleas grow much more vigorously overseas than in their original natural surroundings.

It began to rain and I moved on. Near one of the houses I noticed a plant labelled *Tritonia Goldfinch* which sounded like a bird. I would have liked to see the shape of its flowers and also their colour, but I do not know when it blooms. As I strolled along I noticed more plants from China, such as *Kodreuteria Bipinnata, Spiraea Mollifolia, Allium Gyaneum, Acanthopanax Henryi, Hydragea Sargentiana*. I will not give all the names, for they would convey nothing except to botanists or horticulturists. However, I must mention how interested I was in a small plant with a strong stem and two or three little branches, on each of which were a few large leaves, very artistically spaced. It was labelled *Magnolia Officinalis* from West China. I had never before seen a magnolia like this, and so I made a little sketch of it.

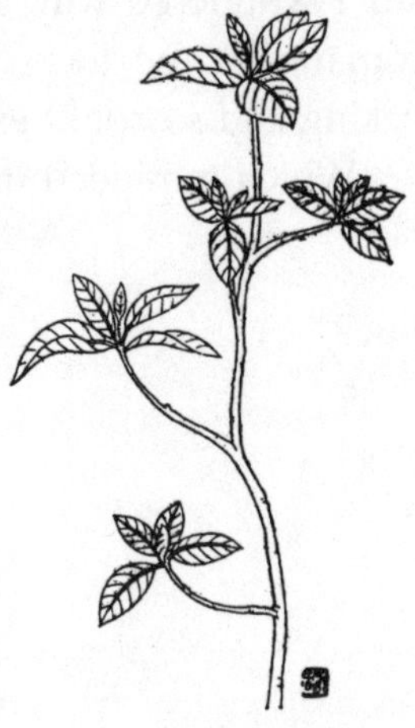

MAGNOLIA OFFICINALIS

The rain stopped suddenly as I came out of the Garden and took my way to Inverleith Public Park, and looking back I saw a beautiful rainbow, which seemed to be quite near me. The Park is a good size and the rainbow spanned it from one end to the other. Then its position changed: one end of it disappeared into a group of trees and the other into the Park. It seemed as though someone hiding in the trees must be controlling the movement of the rainbow by a machine. Some seagulls were flying about and seemed at times to be right inside the rainbow. Then suddenly I saw three people in multi-coloured garments right inside the rainbow at the Park end. I started to walk towards them, but as I approached, both they and the rainbow disappeared.

Before leaving the Park, I looked with interest at a small sandstone monument, on one side of which was a portrait in bas-relief and underneath the words 'John Charles Dunlop, died Feb. 4, 1899'. This unusual type of memorial seemed to me to have a special beauty and pleased me more than many a more imposing statue.

Finally I walked round the little pond, where two children were feeding a pair of swans. They had just thrown their last crumbs, so the swans moved towards me, reminding me of the ducks to whom I had thrown crumbs earlier in the day, and I wondered why the swans did not turn and fly away from me like the ducks. Probably they had finished their love-making and so could give attention to the practical needs of life. Which reminded me that I too needed food.

xiii

Wintry Fascination

'Raining again?'

'Ay, it isn't a very good day for ye.'

I had received the same reply yesterday and the day before, and the day before, and the day before that, and I had come to regard the words as a normal form of greeting and did not hesitate to go out on account of them. I took a tram into town and alighted opposite the Register House, where, even from my limited knowledge of Edinburgh, I knew I should always find some people gazing at the traffic and passers-by, no matter whether it were misty, wet or fine. Of course they would not stand there in torrents of rain, and so I had begun to regard these people as my barometer; if some onlookers were standing there it would not rain heavily for some time—I had found this a fine guide on a number of occasions. Many Edinburgh people seem not to mind a little rain, particularly those who stand at the Register House. In other parts of Britain I had found myself remarkable for my indifference to rain, and I always looked with interest at these kindred spirits and by degrees became quite familiar with the faces of some of them. Yesterday I noticed that one of the group must have cracked a joke, for several of the people leaning on the pedestal of the statue of the Duke of Wellington were rocking with laughter. Three others who had been standing beside the clock on the wall hurried to join the laughing group. It was an interesting sight. I wondered how these people could afford to stand there day after day— perhaps they had something to do with the Register House. To me they were typical Edinburgh characters and I was glad to have noticed them.

REGISTER HOUSE

I crossed the road and joined a small crowd watching people entering and leaving the North British Station Hotel and others going down and up the long flight of steps to Waverley Station. Many people might find it trying to walk up and down these steep steps, particularly when they become slippery after rain, but Edinburgh youngsters seem to regard sliding on them as good fun. I often saw boys jumping up and down there. Once as I returned to Edinburgh from Glasgow and was following the other passengers up the steps, a messenger boy who apparently had a telegram to deliver came dashing down at high speed. It was raining hard and the surface was well washed, and as he slid across one of the landings he slipped and fell flat while his legs shot into the air, just missing the head of an elderly lady who was coming up. She clung to the wall and the heavy boots fortunately missed her by an inch. She turned to the boy and asked if he were hurt. 'Weel, nae baad,' he said, getting up, and had no sooner uttered the words than he dashed off again, sliding as before, and was out of sight in a second. Some passers-by smiled at the lady, who was, of course, unaware of the boy's game.

The rain continued. I had come out with no definite destination in mind, but remembering that the previous night I had wanted to get a clearer view of a certain scene, I walked some way down Leith Street, and found myself where I wished to be. I then realised that it was Regent Bridge which had puzzled me. This is not a bridge over a river or a ravine but over a road far below. It has only one rather narrow arch. I wondered how this gap had originally been made before Edinburgh had any inhabitants. I never think it a waste of time to ponder on the distant past. It fascinates me to think how much human beings can accomplish and how many changes a land has passed through. Many people lament the multitude of changes at present taking place, others clamour for still further changes. But as I stood on the bridge I doubted whether this scene would ever change. I did not know how old it was, but the large building on my right with the curved weather-beaten façade looked very old. It may not have been the scene of any important historical event; it would not be as old as those closes, wynds and courts in the Old Town; nor is it in as prominent a position as the Royal Mile; but it seemed to me to be a building typical of Edinburgh. Its wall was curved to follow the curve of the road and the ground-floor doors were graduated to follow its slope. It was a hotel, but the name sign had faded and I could not read it. I had seen buildings with rounded walls but never before one which

THE REGENT BRIDGE AT NIGHT FROM LEITH STREET

had a concave wall. Before the invention of electric light the rooms must have been very dark, and in the lower ones one must feel very conscious of the dampness of the atmosphere when it rains hard. No doubt they are living-rooms and must always have been occupied and will continue so.

Passing under the bridge I saw a number of Royal Mail vans coming up from the General Post Office. I remembered that it had been pitch dark down there when I had looked at it the night before. People emerged from the road under the bridge as if by magic, those going down simply vanished. Ruskin said, 'No architecture is so haughty as that which is simple'. That was the impression this place made on me.

I debated whether to go up Calton Hill to see Edinburgh through the drizzle or take a tram to Portobello. Before I had made up my mind I was roused by a young boy asking if I wanted to be directed anywhere. Without thinking I said 'No, thank you', and the boy ran over to the other side of the road and vanished in the crowd outside the Station Hotel. I wish I could remember his exact words. The following conversation which I had read in an Edinburgh evening paper came to my mind:

> BOY. I wis stannin' ootside the Post Office this forenoon an' a man gied me tuppence for directin' 'im tae the High Street. Later anither man gied me tuppence for directin' 'im tae Maitland Street.
>
> CHUM. Ye wis lucky.
>
> BOY. No, I wisna', the second man should ha'e gi'en me fourpence, for the distance wis twice as faur.

That boy would certainly have considered himself unlucky with me just then!

The wind was blowing strong gusts from the east. It was so strong that the people standing in front of the Register House seemed to be shivering. My resolution to go up Calton Hill was shaken, and I doubted if I should be able to stand upon the promenade at Portobello. However, I continued to brave the wind and walked on in the face of it. Entering the Old Calton Burying Ground I saw that many of the tombs were protected by a stone wall, not unlike some Chinese tombs, though they were smaller and more compact than ours. I noticed the tomb of David Hume and a monument to Abraham Lincoln, doubtless visited by many American soldiers during the war. Continuing my way I came to St. Andrew's House, a very fine-looking modern building standing by itself, which houses many Government departments. On the opposite side is the Royal High School which I had passed several times but had never seen anybody inside. There seemed no hope of getting in to have a look at it so I did not cross the road, but instead went down a little side-path leading to a green field which I thought must be a public park. Reaching a small iron gate I went through this into the New Calton Burying Ground. Here I found the tombs of Dr. John Brown, author of *Rab and his Friends*, and of other Edinburgh worthies.

VIEW OF NELSON MONUMENT FROM NORTH BRIDGE

The rain began to fall more heavily than before, so I did not linger long and went back by the same path. As it was uphill I walked slowly, with my head raised to the sky. To my surprise I saw in front of me the monument to Robert Burns. It stood solemnly there above me and I stopped to gaze at it in amazement. I was surprised that during my previous visits to Edinburgh I had not seen this impressive monument before; I was amazed that here there was only this one monument, though there are so many others prominently situated in and around Edinburgh. I have always thought that Edinburgh belonged to Sir Walter Scott because wherever I go in the city I seem unable to escape his huge monument. The Castle Hill, Arthur's Seat, Calton Hill and other landmarks have revealed themselves to my mind's eye in many different moods, according to weather and season, never appearing twice alike. But the monument to Sir Walter Scott is always the same. I can see it just as clearly when I am not in Edinburgh as when I am in Princes Street. It tells me that without any doubt Scott was the giant of all Scotsmen, or rather it defies me to argue that he was not. I cannot discuss the subject seriously, for I know so little about this great Scotsman; and even if I knew a great deal, it would be useless for me to argue with any Scotsman about him. But I can make any Scotsman smile when I say that I read a number of Scott's novels in Chinese translations before I could read English. Now as I stood in front of the monument to Robert Burns I compared it with that of Scott. As I said above, the latter proclaims that Scott was a giant because he did so much for Scotland and Scotsmen. This Burns Monument roused different feelings in me. Viewed from ground-level it seemed a simple and unassuming monument which might well be ignored among the many more conspicuous landmarks in Edinburgh. I could not get inside the enclosure and thus was not able to see the carving on it at close quarters nor discover whether it bore a portrait of Burns. But when I looked up at it from the lower level of the New Calton Burying Ground it seemed to me singularly beautiful and serene. Perhaps it should always be looked at in this way. The greatness of Burns is not to be detected on the surface nor with the head, but only from the depth of the Scotsman's heart. Scotsmen share in the triumph of Scott, but with Burns they feel a close kinship.

The rain fell more heavily than ever. Two small trees, one on either side of the path, flanked the monument, which seemed to be sunk in the grey murk of early spring in Edinburgh. It was the 3rd of March 1944. I had been unable to come in time to see Edinburgh in winter, but this seemed near enough. The two little trees were still leafless but their twigs were swaying and nodding in the strong wind. The silhouette of the Burns Monument stood out more clearly as the dark clouds passed, leaving the grey sky as background. Though I could not see the actual movement of the clouds nor the growth of the trees inside their bark, I felt that all my surroundings were alive; even the monument was a monument no longer, but Robert Burns himself. He stood there majestically above the capital of Scotland. Only he could read and interpret what was written on it.

Suddenly a group of small birds flew over the tree-tops towards the monument. Some of them circled round it and some seemed to drop into the warmth of Burns's bosom and be seen no more. What a beautiful revelation of natural friendliness this was to me! It also gave me a wonderful inspiration for a picture—the grey sky, the dark outline of the Burns Monument, the dusky bodies of the birds and the black trunk and branches of the trees, four different shades of colour blending one with another. Such a harmonious winter scene as I love to paint.

Perhaps it is because we Chinese paint in monochrome that I have developed such a keen appreciation of winter, though it is not so much the actual season which delights me as the way in which it sharpens my perceptions. Spring intoxicates the soul; summer slows down one's activities; autumn rouses the feelings; but winter clears the head. Only in winter do we see two sides of Nature as of life. Many people dislike winter and, if they can afford it, 'follow the sun' and thus escape the rigours of the cold; but this is to run away from reality and to lose the intensity of the advent of spring. In winter one hears the cry of birds for food; one sees some of one's fellow-creatures shivering at work; one sees naked trees and the barren landscapes. On the other hand, winter arouses glad hopes of the future. I cannot fail to be attracted by winter's serenity.

The great painters of our T'ang and Sung times painted countless winter scenes, but, possibly because the colours of some of our buildings are out of keeping with winter, our artists have seldom chosen scenes in cities. The serenity of Edinburgh buildings against the winter background fascinates me. 'Winter raises mind to a serious sublimity,' wrote Robert Burns, 'favourable to everything great and noble. There is scarcely any earthly object gives me more—I do not know if I should call it pleasure—but something which exalts me—something which enraptures me—than to walk in the sheltered side of a wood, or high plantation in a cloudy winter day, and hear the stormy wind howling among trees and raving over the plain.' I can add nothing to this. Burns should have been with me at this moment—as in fact he was, standing before me in stone.

My thoughts on Burns went a step further. I am in no position to write an essay on him after the thousands of books and articles already written by well-known authorities. Even if I were foolish enough to begin I should not know enough to finish it. But I began to wonder about his nationality. Certainly this has not been questioned by any previous writer: naturally no Scot would ever dream of doing so. Some time ago I read somewhere that Confucius, China's greatest sage, was a Persian, and that Motse, another great Chinese philosopher, whose work was not translated into any foreign language until some ten years ago, was a German. The author of these suggestions had made a close study of the Chinese race and put forward much evidence from Confucius and Motse to support his statements. They sounded too plausible to be true. Recently I read 'Shakespeare's Legacy' by the late Sir James Barrie in which the wife asserts to her husband that Shakespeare was a Scot from Glen Drumly, so why should I not claim Robert Burns as a Chinese by birth, particularly as I can quote the following poem from a collection of Chinese love-songs of twenty-five centuries ago?

Bonnie is my quiet lassie, supposed to be
Waiting for me at the corner of the city-wall,
I love her but know not where she is.
Scratching my head I pace to and fro.

Fair is my quiet lassie,
Who gave me a crimson reed.
This crimson reed glows
And reflects her beauty that I love.

From the pasture she brought back for me a tender blade,
So beautiful and rare.
It is not that you, the blade, are beautiful,
But you are the gift of my love.

靜女其姝俟我於城隅愛而不見搔首踟躕靜女其孌貽我彤管彤管有煒說懌女美自牧歸荑洵美且異匪女之爲美美人之貽

右詩經之一章

朱門酒肉臭路有凍死骨

右杜甫句

Surely the only difference between this old folk-song and the songs of Burns lies in the language. Perhaps Burns came to live in Scotland at an early age, so that he was able to master the local dialect well enough to express feelings and emotions innate in him from birth. Perhaps he was brought back as a baby from China by some Scottish missionary named Burns, whose adventures were unfortunately left untold in those days when China or Cathay was considered too heathen to have any connection with Scotland.

ROBERT BURNS IN CHINESE DRESS

I do not wish to start an argument, nor to claim that I know anything about Christianity, yet it seems to me that Robert Burns' life and thoughts are more Confucian than Christian. In a letter to 'Clarinda' Burns wrote: 'I firmly believe that every honest upright man, of whatever sect, will be accepted by the Deity.' This phrase, 'every honest upright man', was constantly used by Confucius: his main principle 'The measure of man is man' could not have been better expressed than by Burns' 'A Man's a Man for a' That'. Confucius once said: 'Truth may not depart from human nature. If what is regarded as truth departs from human nature, it may not be regarded as truth.' Burns' lament in 'Man was Made to Mourn' reveals the naked truth of human nature. Burns repeatedly showed his reverence and love for his father in such poems as his 'Epitaph on the Author's Father' and 'My Father was a Farmer', and he followed in his father's footsteps as a ploughman. No genuine Chinese could have been more sincere in his ancestor worship than Burns was. Those of his songs in which he expresses his thoughts on nature, good fellowship, friendship and humanity might have been taken almost word for word from the Analects of Confucius.

Unfortunately, Burns did not live in Scotland at a good time. It was not long after the 'Forty-five and the common people were enduring much hardship and privation. It is difficult to visualise how barely and simply they lived in those days, though, thanks to Burns, we can gain some idea of their mode of existence. Tu Fu of the T'ang Dynasty, who lived in a very troubled time after the Anlushan Rebellion in the ninth century, saw much of the hardship which the simple folk endured, and experienced great privation himself. His works, too, are full of pity and kindness for the poor and anger against the rich. The following two lines sum up Tu Fu's thought:

> The wine and meat lay waste and went bad within the
> red-painted doors,
> Whilst the bones of those who died from cold and
> starvation lay scattered about the road.

Burns' similar thoughts found expression in: 'God knows I'm no saint, but if I could—and I think I do it as far as I am able—I would wipe all tears from all eyes.' Burns was not a happy man. His heart was too deeply attached to the sad side of human life for him to be really gay. But no one can be a true poet who lacks experience of both sides of life. Burns might not have become famous if he had remained in China, as so many of our poets and thinkers have expressed his point of view in one form or another, but none of them has succeeded in wiping away all tears. It was Burns' good fortune to live in Scotland, where, though he may not have been able to wipe away as many tears as he wished, he yet inspired the Scots to value their tears.

One day I confided my thoughts on Burns' nationality to a Scottish friend in Oxford. He at once warned me that if I claimed Burns as a Chinese I should have to be prepared to find every type of Scottish spade, spear and sword thrust through the windows of my room wherever I might stay in Scotland. I laughed and said that that would make me the first and only Chinese Confucian martyr in the world! But it puzzles me how the Scots can be so selfish as to want to keep Burns all to themselves when he himself was always thinking of others. After all, he was but a human being, and his gaiety, gravity, humour and pathos are shared by all other human beings, any one of whom can claim Burns as his or her kinsman. I happened one day to pick up a book entitled *Burns in Germany* by the Rev. W. Mackintosh, honorary member of the Ninety Burns Club, Edinburgh. As the author was a Scot, he did not claim that Burns was a German, but his book may have persuaded many Germans that he was. Burns is one of the universal human beings, in the same category as Confucius, Dante, Shakespeare, Goethe, Ibsen, Tolstoy and many others. I have always declared in my other books that I would like to see all the names of the various nations abolished and all the national boundaries wiped out, leaving only the local place-names. If this could be achieved, I should not bother myself with the question of Burns' nationality and I would be spared the threat of Scottish spades, spears and swords!

On this windy, rainy winter day I gazed at the Burns Monument and penetrated 'the honest, open, naked truth' of the winter scene that Burns loved so much.

ONE OF THE EDINBURGH STREETS

XIV
Friendly Recollections

For many of my pleasant recollections of Edinburgh I am indebted to the late D. P. Heatley, author of the biography of Lord Grey of Falloden under the name of *Politicus,* and former reader in Political and Social Science at Edinburgh University. I first met Mr. Heatley on the island of Eilean Righ, on the west coast near Crinan, Argyllshire, in 1937, when the late Sir Reginald Johnston, one of his pupils, was our host. I did not see him on my first visit to Edinburgh that year, but during my next few visits he and I had many interesting talks. He introduced me to some of his friends and in every way showed me the greatest kindness.

He must have been getting on in years when I saw him in Edinburgh, for he used to tell me of things he remembered happening there fifty years before. He was so masterfully polite that he always insisted on my preceding him, whether we were in a crowded street or stuck in a revolving door. He used to say with a smile that he must look after me while I was in his home town. With my deep-rooted tradition of showing respect to my elders my instinct ran counter to his wishes, which sometimes caused me embarrassment. Fortunately the Edinburgh tram conductors are all very careful and courteous, so that we were always able to walk in a slow and leisurely fashion. Edinburgh is the only city I know in which the trams and buses do not show off to the pedestrians. It is also, I think, the only city where the inhabitants do not appear to be bustling about the whole time. Mr. Heatley died, unfortunately, before I could produce my promised impression of his city. But I hope he will forgive me if I have not recorded our talks and walks quite correctly!

The first place we visited was James Thin's bookshop. Mr. Heatley wanted me to meet Mr. Thin, because he thought his bookshop in Edinburgh to be as renowned as Blackwell's in Oxford. I had actually been in the bookshop the day previously and bought a copy of *Holyrood* by William Moir Bryce, but Mr. Thin was not in on that occasion. Now he received us most cordially in his office. Mr. Thin does not live up to his name; he has a round face with a broad smile, and is undoubtedly a very jolly person. When Mr. Heatley told him that I had met Mr. Blackwell of Oxford, Mr. Thin said that he had once stayed at Mr. Blackwell's country home in Berkshire and been shown the view of the Berkshire downs. 'It is beautiful there', he continued. 'But you know what I mean...' But I must not make trouble between these two benefactors of mine who have helped to sell so many of my books.

We came to speak (I don't remember how) about the English lakes, and I expected this would lead Mr. Thin to discourse upon the Scottish lochs. But it was not so. He said he had actually spent one or two holidays in the Lake District and had read my little book *The Silent Traveller in Lakeland*. He remarked that he had tried unsuccessfully to locate the exact scenes depicted in some of my paintings. Mr. Heatley suggested that perhaps he had not looked at the views from the same angle as I had. Mr. Thin admitted that this was so, adding that he hoped I would use my brush and pen to depict the Scottish mountains and lochs. Talking about views reminded me of a story I had read in *Scottish Anecdotes and Tales* by William Grant:

> A small crofter who resided at the foot of a hill in the North had a cow, but was rather short of grass for her. The honest man, not knowing what to do with the cow, tethered her on the top of the hill, where she got little or nothing to eat but heather. A neighbour, on seeing this, remarked to the crofter, 'Od, yer cow has naething tae eat on the tap o' the hill.' The crofter coolly replied, 'She has nae muckle tae eat, but she has a gran' *view.*'

I did not relate this story word for word, but even though it had nothing to do with what we had been talking about, it did make us all laugh heartily. Mr. Thin even helped me to repeat the words in the local dialect.

Afterwards I was taken to see the old University Building in South Bridge, just opposite Mr. Thin's bookshop. The grey stone of which it was built made the Quadrangle look gloomy and less friendly than those of the Oxford Colleges, which are built of Headington limestone. Mr. Heatley pointed out to me where he had taught and where Sir Reginald Johnston had studied some fifty years before. Then we entered the University Library, where we were shown round by the Librarian, who made the usual apology that most of the valuable things had been stored away for safety for the duration of the war. Later we went upstairs and saw the beautifully proportioned University Hall. It was always used, I was told, for meetings and conferences of the University Staff, of which Mr. Heatley had been for many years a member. As we moved along from one shelf to another, a cigar-burn on an oval table was pointed out to us. This table had belonged to Napoleon, who presumably made the burn when in one of his bad humours. Probably no one would have dared to point it out to him, even if it had been noticed at the time. While I was wondering about this, Mr. Heatley asked how the table had come to the University, but the Librarian did not know. This proved to me that a man famous in history could make things great, but things could not make a man great.

One of the lower shelves was full of Chinese books which had been given to the Library long ago by a Scottish missionary who had returned from China. The Librarian apologised for the dirty appearance of the books, adding that they were very seldom read. 'Chinese', he remarked, 'must be a very difficult language to learn. There is only one person in Edinburgh who can read it well, and none of our Chinese friends who are studying here ever come and look at these books.' I agreed that Chinese was probably more difficult than most languages to learn, but thought it could be learnt well if people would spend as much time on it as we Chinese spend on learning English. Very few Westerners start learning Chinese when they are young, and then only because they have to. With regard to these books, I have noticed similar ones in other libraries and been pleased to see them there; but some of them did not seem worthy of their place on the shelves. Very few libraries have sufficient funds to collect all the good books they should have, so how can it be expected that they would have a good selection of Chinese books, unless the volumes happened to be given as presents?

The books in the Edinburgh University Library were probably of no use to the Chinese students there and therefore they did not waste time on them; but this should not give rise to the idea that they could not read Chinese at all. The Librarian agreed, but pointed out that a number of young Chinese who came to study from Singapore and Malay had actually admitted to him that they could not read and write Chinese. I thought that a good many young Chinese born in America would admit the same. They had been brought up in English-speaking schools and might have had no opportunity to study Chinese. 'It is not easy to be a modern man', I said. 'To study one's mother-tongue is a lifelong job, but now one is expected to know more than one language and to learn about other countries. People of different parts of the world have been brought closer together by modern scientific inventions and by this Second World War. But as a result one's life is made miserable by a succession of never-ending tasks—learning so many different languages. If we don't learn them we cannot understand each other. There has been talk of a universal language which everyone would have to learn to speak and write, but who would dare to agree to such a proposal? To do so would lead one to be considered unpatriotic. My reason won't let me say that I don't want to understand other peoples, but I am really afraid to be a modern man as I don't know how I am going to cope with my study of Russian or Hindustani or even Gaelic!'

Before we left the Library I told my companions how Edinburgh University had trained several people who subsequently served the Chinese Government. The best known of these was the late Ku Hung-Ming, a great scholar and translator of *The Conduct of Life,* whose anecdotes were frequently repeated when he was teaching at the National University of Peking. I also told them that the Chinese Ministry of Education has set up a board of scholars to translate the whole of the *Encyclopaedia Britannica* into Chinese.

I should here like to thank the Librarian again for his kindness in showing us around.

'I'm very glad to meet "The Silent Traveller"', said Dr. Meikle of the National Library of Scotland, as he came into his office to shake hands with me when we called on him by Mr. Heatley's arrangement. He was obviously working very hard, but his fresh, friendly, smiling face showed no sign of weariness. I have noticed the same cheerfulness in many Scottish people and it impressed me very much. Someone said that it was due to the bracing climate of Edinburgh. But I think that to show a cheerful face one must have a cheerful heart. Dr. Meikle explained that owing to the war there was a great shortage of staff and only eight people carrying on with all the jobs in the Library. He then said that he had never had the pleasure of meeting Mr. Strickland Gibson, keeper of the Bodleian Library at Oxford, though they corresponded for many years. He thought I must have met Gibson as I was living in Oxford, and I agreed that he was a friend of mine. No author, whether good or bad, can escape the notice of these two men, because a copy of every new book published in Britain must be presented to the Bodleian and to the National Library of Scotland if asked for. It was really amazing Dr. Meikle and Mr. Gibson could remember the name of authors so well.

After showing us the reading-room and some interesting old bookshelves, Dr. Meikle took us to a hall, which has four pillars in its central part. It was not a big hall and all its windows were shuttered; it was lit, not very brightly, by electric light, and this may have made the hall look rather small. There was a long counter with boxes on it, probably containing the indices. David Hume was the librarian at the time that the four big pillars were constructed. He wanted to become a librarian so that he could always have access to books. Sir Walter Scott did the same. Once Boswell took Dr. Johnson to meet David Hume there, and they had a heated argument about the library system, of which Dr. Johnson was not in favour. Dr. Meikle explained that we were standing on the exact spot where Dr. Johnson and Boswell stood. But *we* were not arguing. Dr. Meikle and Mr. Heatley were great friends and had a lot to say to each other. I was living up to my silent reputation. Anyway, Heatley is no Boswell, and I am far from being a Dr. Johnson.

A MAN LED BY A BEAR 

I recalled the witticism of Henry Erskine, the well-known Edinburgh advocate, at the time of Dr. Johnson's visit to Edinburgh. After being introduced to him and talking to him for some time, he slipped a shilling unobtrusively into Boswell's hand and whispered, 'Thank you for the sight of your English bear.' Mrs. Boswell is said to have had a pretty wit too. On one occasion after a visit from Johnson she said, 'I have often seen a bear led by a man, but I never saw a man led by a bear.' I have heard of a Russian being portrayed as a bear, but not an Englishman. Perhaps Dr. Johnson was a naturalised Russian, just as I suggested in another chapter that Robert Burns might be a Chinese. But I thought with a smile that someone might like to slip a threepenny bit into Mr. Heatley's hand and say, 'Thank you for the sight of your Chinese giant panda.'

A CHINESE GIANT PANDA ON GEORGE IV BRIDGE

We moved to another quarter of the building, where I was shown a facsimile letter of Mary Queen of Scots. The original was put away in safety. 'It was written at Fotheringay', said Dr. Meikle, 'on February 8th, 1587, only six hours before her execution. Yet there is no sign of trembling or weakness in the writing. What a wonderful character she had!' The letter was certainly well composed and the writing gave no hint of what was about to happen: no one can deny that Mary Stuart had great courage. It was her destiny to live in peculiar circumstances during a violent period of history. If she had had her way with John Knox and Queen Elizabeth, if she had borne no son to become King of England, Edinburgh might have made a very different impression on me. I would not have had the pleasure of looking at this letter. Historians can only deal with facts, but I cannot accept their easy criticisms of historical events and persons, particularly not their condemnation of Mary Queen of Scots. I doubt if she really wanted to be a queen, or anything more than a perfectly normal, likeable human being. There was a pause after Dr. Meikle's words, to which Mr. Heatley only murmured approval. Doubtless their thoughts were quite different from mine.

Presently we came to a stone statue of Sir Walter Scott. Dr. Meikle mentioned that it had been done by a mason who had no knowledge of sculpture and that it was considered by the Scott family to be an excellent likeness. A number of artists had seen it and had expressed great interest in the Scottish design of the drapery behind the statue but had made no comment on the statue itself. At the suggestion of professional jealousy in his words Dr. Meikle smiled, and Mr. Heatley and I smiled with him.

A writing-case and many other things that had belonged to Sir Walter were shown to us, and I began to feel dazed. Then Dr. Meikle asked one of his staff to take down a box in which a number of Scott's manuscripts were kept. This great privilege moved me deeply. I was told to sit down and go through them myself. Many of them were copies of Scottish ballads and folk-songs which Scott had written out for his aunt. Sir Walter used to give his fly-pages to his friends as presents, and that was why those in the box were not connected with each other. 'Only yesterday', Dr. Meikle continued, 'I was shown a most remarkable forgery of one of these pages.' Mr. Heatley commented on the limits to which man would go. I then said that forgery of handwriting and painting had been going on in my own country for centuries. We treasure a piece of calligraphy just as much as a painting, and there has always been a great demand for examples of a good hand or from a famous person. Human nature is the same the world over; what has been practised in China will be found in other countries as well.

What attracted me most were the first few pages of the manuscript of *Waverley,* written in a clear, careful hand. As I am very interested in Chinese calligraphy, on which subject I have written quite a long book, and as I have been studying English handwriting, though so far without learning very much about it, I naturally looked at these pages very carefully. The Scottish ballads and folk-songs had presumably been written out by Scott at odd times, whereas these few pages of *Waverley* must have been written without interruption. I hope I am right in thinking that the heavy downward strokes in each letter and the careful finish given to each word were signs of his strong-willed character, while the lack of mistakes or signs of weariness were a remarkable indication of what manner of man Scott was. Dr. Meikle told me that the whole manuscript of the novel went to the printer with only one correction. How many authors of today could do this? The fact that many modern works are dictated and typed shows a decline of interest in calligraphy, no doubt, but will perhaps save librarians of the future from being bothered by forgeries.

I remember reading somewhere that Scott was a cheerful, easygoing, temperamental youth and full of pranks. Lame though he was, he climbed every dangerous hill-summit, and knew the recesses of Arthur's Seat and Salisbury Crags by heart before he knew his Latin grammar. In the course of schoolboy fights and snowballing contests he got to know a

THE CASTLE IN THE EARLY MORNING, FROM THE GRASSMARKET

whole gang of little urchins, with whom he took many a hard knock. It was amazing that he could later produce page after page of such neat handwriting. One's mature character cannot be judged from one's childhood.

It is said that Scott began to write *Waverley* on a sudden impulse after he had already become famous as a lawyer in Edinburgh. When he had written half the book, he gave it to his most trusted critic to read, and was advised not to risk his reputation with it. So the MS. was tossed into a drawer and lay there for years untouched. Then one day another friend came to borrow some fishing tackle, and in searching for this Scott came across the bundle of MS. and could not resist reading it through. He came to the conclusion that it was not as bad as he had been led to think before, and he settled down to complete the book. This was the origin of *Waverley* as we know it now: the whole thing a series of chances apparently. I felt very fortunate in having the pleasure of reading the first pages in the author's own hand. The friend who came to borrow the fishing tackle deserves thanks from all readers of *Waverley*. However, it was not only chance that brought *Waverley* into being. Even if he had not found the bundle of written pages in the drawer, Scott would have written it in the end. According to our tradition, there is an invisible divinity which shapes man's ends. This is like the mysterious force which determines the destiny of all Nature's creatures—which ensures, for instance, that no cat can be a dog. Scott was destined to be *the* Scottish writer. When I closed the box, I sat for a moment with my eyes closed. Dr. Meikle roused me by saying that Sir Walter Scott and Robert Louis Stevenson used to tell their stories in front of the big fireplace upstairs before they made them into books. He then asked Mr. Heatley to take me to see the beautiful hall of the Signet Library. I can never sufficiently thank Dr. Meikle.

As suggested, we soon entered the great hall in the south-west corner. It was indeed a fine hall with its handsome ceiling of dark oak still in its original condition. Here another friend of Mr. Heatley, Dr. Malcolm, greeted him at the Signet Library. After being introduced, Dr. Malcolm pointed out to me the beautiful balcony round the top hall decorated in blue and gilt in seventeenth-century French style. I was surprised by the great contrast between the dark exterior and the brilliant interior. Dr. Malcolm showed us a number of things, one which I found particularly interesting being an early horn-book for children, on which were printed simple words and drawings similar to the Chinese square characters with illustrations which were formerly used for teaching our children. 'In the old days these were sold for a penny each,' Dr. Malcolm said, 'but now they would fetch thirty pounds apiece.' Certainly the value of things increases with time, just as the work of an artist is often worth more after his death.

Then we were shown Scott's sofa, which he used in 39 Castle Street and which had been bequeathed to the Library. There was no objection raised when I went to sit on it for a minute; in fact, I was invited to do so. I blushed as I recalled the whim I had had to sit on the Provost's seat in the chapel of Queen's College, Oxford, and how my friend had stopped me. This sounds silly, but I have indulged in similar childish conduct at various times in my life. But I confess that in some ways I am glad to be still a child at heart, otherwise I would have worried myself to death by taking too serious a view of many inexplicable things happening in the world to-day. 'Love of knowledge is akin to wisdom', said Confucius.[1] 'Strenuous attention to conduct is akin to compassion. Sensitiveness to shame is akin to courage.' Have I not shown courage in trying to sit on the Provost's seat in Queen's College Chapel as well as on Scott's sofa? And yet courage invites only sneers from many pompous individuals.

There were a number of engravings on the walls of the staircase, some of which depicted Scott and his friends in Court scenes as well as in more informal moods. One big

1 Translated by Ku Hungming

picture containing a great many figures appeared to depict a very jolly but somewhat confused scene in the Great Hall of the Parliament House. A young man with a long gown was shown being dragged into the hall. No doubt Scott also figured in the picture. But I could not bring myself to ask either Dr. Malcolm or Mr. Heatley—who were engaging in a talk in front of an old map of Edinburgh—what it was about, because my head was really saturated with Scott and would not hold any more information about him.

I remember that soon after my arrival in London in 1933 I met the late Sir James Stewart Lockhart, former Governor of Hong Kong and Commissioner of Wei-hai-wei, who told me that I should go to Scotland, and of course visit Edinburgh, and of course see the Scott Monument in Princes Street. Later, during several visits to Scotland, I have found that in nearly every place in which I stayed there were copies of Scott's works or some connection with his life, and that almost every beauty-spot in Scotland is connected in some way either with Scott himself or with his stories. Once I was told that Scott was to Scotland what Shakespeare was to England, but from my little experience I must say that one might be able to leave England without hearing of Shakespeare but never Scotland without hearing of Scott. The Scott Monument is indeed most impressive. There are many big and imposing monuments in various parts of the world, but none of them, I feel, could make such an impression on one as it does. In fact, it always had the effect of making me bow my head instead of looking at the top of it as I passed. It was as if I murmured to myself, 'I know you all right, Sir Walter. Please don't try to remind me of you.' I have found it possible to pick a Scot out of a number of Britishers by simply mentioning the name 'Sir Walter Scott'. The one who responds to my words is the Scot. But I could not identify an Englishman by simply mentioning Shakespeare; that has to be done by other means, which it would be out of place to mention here. I must confess I find it interesting that

Scott should be a Scot. I like the sound of 'Scott' as I have a number of friends with this name.

All the books on the shelves were about law and were beyond me. Before we said goodbye, Dr. Malcolm told Mr. Heatley that a friend of his would like to see him, and in a minute or two Sir Ernest Wedderburn came in and was introduced to me. He told me that he had a relative living in Oxford, but had not visited him for some time. After he and Mr. Heatley had had a good talk, Sir Ernest suggested that I should sign the Library's Visitors' Book. It was soon produced, still in paper wrapping, and Sir Ernest said that it had only just come back from the King and Queen. Their Majesties' signatures on the first page were shown to us, and Mr. Heatley remarked how like King George VI's signature was to that of his father. I was overwhelmed with this honour and signed my name in Chinese as well as in English. Sir Ernest watched with a smile as I wrote in Chinese, and Dr. Malcolm looked at it for a while and then commented that anyway it could not be forged. After we went out, I said to Mr. Heatley, 'Dr. Malcolm is a fine librarian whose mind is always on his job!'

MCEWAN HALL

Mr. Heatley wanted to take me to see the McEwan Hall at Teviot Row. We went there one morning but at first could not find the entrance. An elderly man standing near by showed us where it was, but we found it locked. However, as we were turning away, a man with a smiling face came to open the door for us. After switching on the lights, the man began to tell us something about the Hall, which was the generous gift of Mr. William McEwan. It was built about fifty years ago, costing about £200,000 in those days of cheap labour. It took more than five years to build and can hold two thousand people. He pointed out the ceiling, on which were painted figures representing branches of study in the University. Most of them were female figures, and it occurred to me that artists of the Western civilisations use the female figure to represent almost anything. Possibly the origin of this is the nine muses of Greek mythology.

Nearly every word spoken by our guide produced an echo in the Hall, which I thought must be a disadvantage for audience and lecturer alike. I was assured, however, that when the Hall was packed with people the echo was not so apparent. I thought the architect might have tried to avoid it, but perhaps it had been done intentionally.

The old man to whom we were listening was presumably the keeper of the Hall and he had a lot to say. I was more interested in the manner in which he related some of the stories than in their matter, because he had a very colourful and distinctive Scottish accent. I must admit that I could not always follow what he said, though he was obviously trying hard to make himself comprehensible to me. In this he was unlike the saleswomen in the shops along Princes Street, who seem able to change from a Scottish accent to an English one at a moment's notice. Both in the West End Bookshop and at Elliot's I have had the experience of being first addressed in Scottish dialect to test if I were studying at the University of Aberdeen or St. Andrews, then being spoken to in the accents of London's West End—not those of the East End, of course, even though my face might have induced them to try that too. I don't mean to boast of my limited knowledge of various dialects, but merely to illustrate one of the things I have enjoyed in Edinburgh. It is not surprising that there are so many different dialects in China considering how many are to be heard in the small area of the British Isles. Although we have many dialects—often wrongly referred to as different languages—there is only one form of written Chinese. But in Scotland some words are not only pronounced differently from the English but spelled in a different way too.

But to return to the old keeper of McEwan Hall. Unlike those official guides who tell stories for a living, or some of the old college servants in Oxford, who give an air of knowing too much before they even say a word, he put himself right into the stories he was relating and told them in a very genuine manner. I think this is the best way of story-telling and the Scottish people are very good at it, especially Highland peasants. Perhaps that is why Scotland has produced such remarkable story-tellers as Sir Walter Scott and Robert Louis Stevenson.

The old keeper said that the most famous events to take place in the Hall were the Rectorial Addresses. He told us what happened when Earl Beatty came to take up his Rectorship of Edinburgh University. At either side of the gallery a number of students had concealed a well-made ship, attached to cords. When these were pulled the ships moved together, and when they collided in the middle of the hall, just in front of the speaker, there was a loud explosion. This was a signal for some confusion and more laughter than had ever been heard in the Hall before. 'But his lordship is a good sportsman,' said the keeper, 'and he went on with his speech unmoved.' He added that the high spirits of the students were not easy to cope with. I must confess I do not know whether or not the Chancellor of Oxford University gives an address when taking up his appointment. Perhaps Edinburgh students have no boat races or regattas at which to make merry and so have their rags during the Rectorial Addresses.

Before we left, the old keeper produced the Visitors' Book and asked for my signature. First he showed me that of Anna May Wong, the Chinese film actress. I was struck by the fact that he remembered her visit to Edinburgh some time before the war.

On only one of my previous visits to Edinburgh did I fail to see Mr. Heatley. He was away staying with a friend in Suffolk when I went to give a talk on Chinese painting at the Exhibition of Chinese Art in the National Gallery at the Mound. I have many pleasant recollections of this visit. Soon after my arrival I was informed that the Marquis and Marchioness of Linlithgow were going to visit the Exhibition, and was asked by those in charge to be there if I could. Naturally I agreed. The Marquis had another engagement and could not come, but the Marchioness arrived at the appointed time. At first she was shown round by one of the officers from the Scottish Region of the British Council. An army officer who accompanied the Marchioness exclaimed to me, 'My God! What a fine horse!' when he noticed a huge brown pottery horse in the middle of one big hall. I agreed, and suggested that as the officer had his riding habit on he might like to ride it. He winked at me and said he would not mind taking it home with him. He went on to say that he had always understood that Chinese horses were very small, like Mongolian ponies. I told him that this particular horse was probably modelled in the T'ang period, about the eighth century, when China had many visitors from the Middle East. 'So you had Arab horses much earlier than we did', he commented; 'but where is your Arab stock now?' I replied that I did not know and added there were very few records of Chinese families keeping horses and no horse-racing took place in ancient China...

Presently I had to explain to the Marchioness some points about Chinese porcelain of the early Ching period. She soon found out that I was a friend of her brother, Sir William Milner, Bt., who had sent her a copy of my book *The Silent Traveller in the Yorkshire Dales* while she was in India, and she told me that I should write to Sir William about our meeting. We went round all the cases containing porcelain of different periods. When the Marchioness said she liked the Sung period best I told her that Chinese porcelain-making reached its zenith at that time. I went on: 'At first people in the West were most enthusiastic about porcelain of the early Ching period, such as that of Kang Hsi, Chien Lung and others. But as soon as they had seen some Sung vases these were at once preferred. This was only natural, because the Sung porcelain achieved *harmony* and *simplicity* in design, colour and quality. No improvement on the achievements of the Sung period could be effected. In the Ming period many good imitations of Sung vases were produced. In the Ching period elaborate decorations were added, but these did not improve the porcelain, though they look very pleasing if there are no Sung porcelains near by with which to compare them. Unfortunately there are not many Sung vases to be found now.'

After we had looked at some of the other exhibits, such as jades, lacquer, embroidery and paintings, we came to a little room where a number of my own works were being shown. The Marchioness at once remarked that I was lucky to have a room exclusively for my own works. I smiled, but said nothing, though I silently whispered my thanks to the authorities, Major A. A. Longdon, Director of the Fine Arts Department of the British Council, and Dr. K. C. Yeh, Director of the Chinese Ministry of Information, who must have made such an arrangement possible.

This exhibition of Chinese art, containing over seven hundred different exhibits, aroused great interest in Edinburgh, and it was very well attended.

On the evening when I gave a lecture there, I was surprised to face a very crowded house. When I mentioned that Arthur's

Seat looked to me more like an elephant than a lion, a cry of 'Yes' came from somewhere in the audience, causing much laughter. Although I knew that many present would not agree with me, I was glad to hear one sign of approval. I could not believe that it had come from any Scotsman, and so it proved to be. After the lecture a young lady rushed up to speak to me. She said she came from New Zealand and that she had had the same impression of Arthur's Seat as I had and had been very pleased to hear me say so. Perhaps this odd coincidence was due to the fact that New Zealand and China are close neighbours.

Two more incidents on this occasion moved me deeply. I was surrounded by people anxious to ask questions, and eventually an elderly man who had been patiently waiting without saying a word carefully took out from his pocket a carved ivory snuff-box. 'This has been in my family for years and years', he said with child-like pride. 'I just wanted to show it to you.' As he was putting it back in his pocket, someone interrupted and asked for how much he would sell it. 'I would never sell it', he replied. It was, of course, a Chinese snuff-box. It was of such great sentimental value to him that it made me feel sentimental too. I gazed at him with a smile but could say nothing!

It was now getting late and I had to be on my way. As I came out of the lecture-room an old couple waylaid me. They appeared to belong to my parents' generation. The old gentleman had white hair and a thick white moustache and carried a large parcel under one arm. His hands shook as he slowly unwrapped one paper covering after another, eventually revealing four small Chinese scroll paintings done in black ink with a few touches of colour. 'We want you to tell us what they are', said the wife. The husband said that the pictures had been brought back from China by his father, who had been a sailor, and that he had kept them carefully ever since. Husband and wife then explained together that they had come into Edinburgh from the country and were staying with a friend for the night, especially to have their pictures interpreted. They were very eager and sincere, and I was glad to be able to gratify their wish and tell them the story of each picture in turn.

People who know a little about Chinese painting are inclined to jeer at commoner pieces of work. But I did not examine these little scrolls for their artistic value, which was certainly small, and I doubt if even their owners thought much of them on that account. They treasured them out of filial regard for the parent who had brought them back from the East. I was touched by the trouble they had taken, first to preserve the pictures through many years, then to bring them a considerable distance to the lecture to discover from a native of China what they meant. I wondered wistfully whether, if I were to take back to China some souvenirs of Scotland, my children would preserve them, and, in their old age, trouble to inquire of some British lecturer what they meant. I fear not. Filial regard is a matter of tradition: and although Chinese civilisation has a very long history, for the last one hundred years it has been very far from stable and tradition has weakened. Possibly my feelings on this occasion were subjective, but as I looked at the two gentle smiling faces before me my eyes filled unaccountably with tears!

XV
Unwanted Intrusion

Not only is Edinburgh a royal capital and the scene of many noble deeds, but its hilly parts, such as Arthur's Seat, Calton Hill, Blackford Hill, the Pentland Hills, and its seashore along the Firth of Forth, particularly at Portobello, which can easily be reached by tramcar, are resorts for tourists and holiday-makers. I had been to Portobello once before, but on a very stormy day when I found myself unable to brave the elements and reach the sea. My second visit was on a morning in early June. Alighting from the tram near St. Philip's Church, I turned my back on the town and walked straight to the Promenade. It was a sunny morning, but chilly as an Edinburgh June can be. I was happy to be there before the crowds. Staring at the great expanse of water, I drew a tremendously deep breath as though by reflex action. 'The sea! The sea!' I murmured ecstatically. Everyone knows that lift of the spirit when one moves suddenly out of confined streets into a wide expanse. The people within my range of vision were so few that the Promenade seemed empty. My sensation recalled two lines from a poem on 'The South Sea' by T'sao Sung of the T'ang Dynasty:

The sameness makes me realise the meaning of
'remoteness';
Having difficulty in distinguishing the sky from the sea
I understand what is meant by 'broadness'.
This sensation dispelled the chill of the early morning.

Sauntering along I thought of the Chinese attitude to the sea and of my own in particular. Before I came to live in the British Isles I knew very little of the sea. The same could be said of the majority of my countrymen, millions of whom, born in the vast Chinese hinterland, never see the sea in all their lives. So, for us, the sea has remained a vague thing, a mystery. It is seldom described by our literary men, unlike our mountains and rivers, which are an ever-living source of inspiration. But in our ancient classics it is mentioned often. I have already told the story of the 'First Emperor' of the Ch'in Dynasty, builder of the Great Wall, who wanted to build a stone bridge over the East Sea in order to cross it and see the place where the sun rose. He may actually have attempted this. He failed because he could not master water as he could master dry land. Under his tyrannical dictatorship endless lives were sacrificed to the building of the Wall, which is now deemed one of the 'wonders' in the world. He might have driven his people to this fresh task in the sea, but with no result. Had he built his bridge, we Chinese might permanently have acquired a very different idea of the sea. I wonder which nation would then have ruled the waves? The 'New' Continent of America might have been discovered, not by Columbus but by some Chinese two thousand years or more ago, and the United States would not now be a 'new' world! Fate ruled otherwise, and nobody again attempted to imitate the First Emperor of Ch'in. In the succeeding centuries we Chinese almost forgot the sea.

With a few exceptions, the first Chinese did not struggle for existence by the sea, but are supposed to have had their early beginnings round the valley of the Yellow River far inland, where the fertile soil and agreeable climate were favourable for work.

It thus came to be accepted that those who dwelt inland were cultured, while those who lived by the sea were more or less barbarian. Once, after trying many times in vain to convince a number of kings and dukes from different states by his arguments, Confucius said in a tone of disgusted disappointment he would go to sea on a raft, meaning that he would rather live among the people by the sea than where he was. As the Chinese way of life has been dominated by the sayings of Confucius, it might have been felt from an early time that we Chinese could not degrade ourselves by living near the sea.

It is a curious fact that very few of the literary figures of China have known anything about the sea, except those who had a glimpse of it from some high mountain peak. And thus there is very little about the sea in Chinese literature. However, our admiration for mountains and rivers is reflected in our landscape painting, which has been our highest form of artistic expression since the fourth century, long before such art blossomed in the West.

Our lack of knowledge of the sea is proverbial! The following episode took place only fifty years ago. During the last Manchu Dynasty a Councillor named Mei Shou-chi accompanied our envoy, H. E. Liu Chih-tien, to France and England, and afterwards returned to report to the Minister of State, Chi Shih-Yin. After introductions the latter said: 'You must have endured great hardships during more than four years on the terrifying waves. Aren't you happy to see land again?' Mei replied, 'The journey from China to England took little more than a month. After that we went ashore and did not go back to the sea until the mission was completed.' Chi Shih-Yin was astonished to learn that there was land in England and inquired whether there were also dwelling-houses and edible crops as in China. Hiding a smile, Mei answered, 'Yes, indeed'. Chi Shih-Yin smiled and said, 'Now I have learnt something new. I used to think of our foreign envoys as generally living on board ship the whole year round and seeing no land at all!

Now I know I am mistaken.' Peking laughed over the mistake, but did not profit by it even after China had twice been defeated by the powerful British Navy! Perhaps this is the reason why China has never developed her extensive sea-coasts, a fact which of course the people of the West, and particularly the British, could never understand!

Thus it was that I myself had no knowledge of the sea until at the age of twenty I made my first voyage to Hong Kong, Canton and Hainan Island. Although I had many adventures on the trip, I cannot claim that I learned much about the sea beyond the fact that it gave me an uneasy feeling inside, for the boat was small and the weather bad. It was in 1933, when I travelled from China to France and then to England via the Indian Ocean and the Mediterranean, that I had my first real experience of the sea. After many years' stay in this country I have come to appreciate the importance of the sea to the British people. They accept the sea in whatever mood it happens to be, as their very existence is bound up with it.

Nearly everybody has been to the sea at some time, not least the men of letters, and a great deal of literature about the sea is produced each year. Seascapes also have featured prominently in the painting of the West. I think I am not far wrong in saying that as a rule Western civilisation, taking Egypt, Greece and Italy as its centres, grew up in coastal areas. It is thus quite different from the civilisation of China. I wonder whether the two civilisations, land and sea, will ever merge. Land civilisation produces a rational people because they do not all the time have to battle for existence; while sea civilisation, involving a constant struggle, produces a scientific race and one that is more stable. Inevitably, therefore, the latter will overcome the former, I fear, and has indeed already done so. Personally, I consider that Chinese civilisation stands at present at the cross-roads, and I feel we should find ways and means of accepting the approach of the civilisation from the sea, particularly in view of our long seaboard.

It has taken me several years' residence in England to become really acquainted with the sea, but I now love it whenever I see it. Milton wrote: 'Yet winds to seas are reconcil'd at length, and sea to shore.' How much one's environment can mould one's mind! But Longfellow sang:

> 'Wouldst thou'—so the helmsman answered,
> 'Learn the secret of the sea
> Only those who brave its dangers
> Comprehend its mystery!'

Shall we Chinese ever be able to become sea-minded if we do not ourselves try to become helmsmen?

Suddenly a voice saying 'Good morning' roused me from my thoughts. I raised my head quickly and returned the greeting. The voice belonged to one of two elderly ladies, who told me that she had for some years been a missionary in China. 'I love the seaside of Ching-tao', she said, 'and of Pei-tai-ho too—both in Northern China, you know.' Not wishing to appear impolite, I replied as best I could. She would never be able to guess what my thoughts had been. Then, thinking that I might not have been able to understand what she said, she began to speak in Chinese. This did not make me any more anxious to continue the conversation, but I went on smiling, ostensibly at her but really at my own thoughts. In a few minutes she bid me good-bye and, with her friend, turned off to catch a tram for the city.

The Promenade was clean and the air was fresh. Occasionally the wind blew on my ear the sound of the waves beating against the shore. As the tide was very low, the sound was soft but clear like a gentle tune. At one moment it appeared to welcome my presence by imitating my surname: 'Chi-iang, chi-iang… chi-iang'; at another as though it were crying 'ph-woo, ph-woo… ph-woo', to keep away an unwelcome intruder. However, it did not seem to matter to me whether it was a welcome or the reverse. Certainly it did not matter to the waves whether I was there or not. They had been making the same sound day after day, night after night, year after year and century after century, loudly or softly according to the sea's mood. It was my own self-importance which made me think the sea was speaking to me.

A door in the block of buildings on my left opened and someone came out to polish the brass. I remembered that cleaning door-brasses was a profession I had so far only encountered in Edinburgh. For several mornings during my first visit I had noticed a man who handled the brass on one door for a while, then, without opening it, moved on to the next door, the brass of which he handled in the same way, and so on for a third, fourth and fifth door. This struck me as strange and I thought that the man was either playing some game or else was an eccentric, probably the latter. Later when I was asked to deliver a lecture on Chinese painting, of which I spoke in the previous chapter, I had lunch beforehand in a friend's house. One of the guests asked me whether China still had many eccentrics and whether they were still revered, as he thought it the only country in the world where this was the case. Pleasantly surprised, I replied, 'Why, yes. China regards those who study or read too much as eccentrics, and as it is our tradition to revere the learned, these over-studious persons deserve the respect due to them.' The guest sighed and then remarked, 'What a good country to live in! Edinburgh used to be like that, but now, if one were considered eccentric, one could not live here. Modern society regards as outcasts those who do not button up their clothes properly or walk in the usual manner.' I felt that I did not rightly understand the word 'eccentric'. However, I went on: 'The modern way of living has been largely influenced by machines. If the machines were not kept oiled and in good working order they would stop and modern life would be disorganised. I do not know whether China is fortunate to have so many eccentrics, but they certainly keep our nation out of step with the rest of the world!

By the way,' I continued, 'I see that Edinburgh still has many interesting characters like those described in Sir Walter Scott's novels; for instance, the man who handles the door brasses one after the other...' I went on to describe the man I noticed in the mornings. No sooner had I finished speaking than guests and host burst out laughing, and although I was somewhat bewildered I joined in too. The guest who had previously spoken to me became very eloquent on the subject and, though I cannot remember the exact words, the sense was as follows: 'Edinburgh is very proud of the brasses on her dwelling-houses. They date back to olden times and they are still polished every day by this professional cleaner. It is a delight to every native of Edinburgh, as it must also be to every visitor to Edinburgh, to see those shining brasses sparkling above every doorstep in the streets.' I felt embarrassed that I had failed temporarily to live up to my name. However, I would not have known that there was a man whose profession it was to clean the brasses in Edinburgh every day, had I kept silent. Certainly I have never seen elsewhere such shining brasses as I saw in grey Edinburgh, and those along the Promenade at Portobello looked brighter than ever in the morning sun!

I wondered where the young lads had come from who were now playing and jumping about close to the water's edge. I could see them standing out in silhouette, small but clear, against a background of white-crested green sea. It looked like a painting, for though everything was moving incessantly, the general effect remained the same, though the positions of the boys moved slightly. They were such small black dots compared with the huge expanse. But though they occupied so little space in the picture, the fact that they were undoubtedly the most important things in sight I found pleasing. From this I learned a principle for the composition of pictures: the most important feature will always stand out, no matter how small, while it is futile to attempt to exaggerate either in size or in colour anything which is not the main feature.

Undoubtedly the sea was deep green in colour, at least so it appeared to me at the moment. This seemed contrary to what I read about the dark blue of the sea, but I thought it might be due to the combination of the perfect blue sky with the yellow sands, since these two colours combine to make green. But the sky was not entirely blue. Far away on the horizon appeared a tiny white cloud which gradually grew bigger till it resembled a vast sheet or a huge sponge, and moved into the middle of the sky, shedding a dark shadow on the surface of the sea. I could not see the actual movement of the cloud, but its shadow was like the hands of some heavenly mother caressing the little white heads of the sea, murmuring meanwhile through the waves, 'Keep moving steadily, nothing will stop you and no one should turn back.' It seemed a prophecy for my future!

At the same time the sunbeams shone on the white-caps of the waves, creating various degrees of light and shade. Two lines from a poem written by the illustrious Emperor Tai Tsung of T'ang Dynasty when watching the sea-waves from a high mountain peak in spring may well describe the scene:

> The clouds spread different colours as they swept over
> the sea;
> The sun's beams pierce the waves, breathing light
> through all.

無地不同方覺遠
共天難別始知寬
右唐曹松南海句

拂潮雲佈色穿浪
日舒光
右唐太宗春日望海句

朝遊孤嶼南暮戲
孤嶼北所以孤嶼
鳥與公盡相識
右唐韓愈孤嶼詩

Or perhaps an old Chinese phrase 'yu-jih' ('bathing the sun' or 'the-sun-is-taking-a-bath') is a more poetic description of the scene. Some deity was moving the heavenly body up and down in the water to cleanse it, after which it shone more brilliantly than ever, throwing off its rays in all directions. The youngsters silhouetted at the water's edge were the immortal attendants at this ceremony! I was glad to have this old Chinese phrase interpreted to me by this beautiful scene.

Being but an ignorant man, I was anxious to discover what those attendants had in their hands for their master's use after his bath. So I went down to the sands and walked towards them. The soft feeling of the sand against the soles of my feet gave me a strange sensation and I began to wonder if it was firm ground I was treading on. My body seemed too heavy and my shoulders to be carrying too big a load. But as I quickened my steps my feet felt more secure and my body lighter as though the load had fallen from me. Life never goes straight along, for no one could be entirely without some burden of responsibility which gives a zigzag course to his progress along the path of life. However, it was a good thing to be free of the load for the moment.

As I approached the boys I could hear them laughing; perhaps they were pleased to find that I was not a heavy-looking man after all. Anyway, I felt almost as though I were one of them. Then I saw they were not looking at me, and had perhaps not even noticed my presence. They were moving about without set purpose. Two of them were jumping from stone to stone and occasionally the foot of one would slip off into the sea and get wet, which was the signal for more laughter. The others were playing games which I did not know. Some were gathering shells, others throwing them at each other. I would have liked to join their play, but I hesitated to intrude myself in case I should not be wanted. So for a while I remained standing on a small stone close to the water's edge.

The whole scene which I had watched from the Promenade had changed. I repeatedly drew deep breaths as the waves came towards me and exhaled as they receded. Sometimes my hands instinctively raised and lowered themselves as I breathed in and out, as though I were doing exercises in a gymnasium. Then I imagined I was holding a long bar with strong cords attached at either end and began to pull and push it, following the movement of the waves.

THE SEASHORE AT PORTOBELLO

The white-caps of the waves had grown bigger; I felt excited as I performed these exercises.

I could now see very little land apart from the actual spot on which I was standing. Everywhere there was water. I wondered whether I or anybody else had ever thought that there could be so much water on earth—or rather in the world. Geologists say that water occupies two-thirds and land only one-third of the world. The little bit of land on which I was standing was negligible. I myself was as nothing there. Yet there might be someone standing on the Promenade who thought of me as a royal attendant waiting beside the bath-tub of an immortal king—the sun—as I myself had previously regarded these boys. Once again I became conscious of a sense of self-importance and laughed to myself.

QUEEN MARY'S BATH IN RAIN

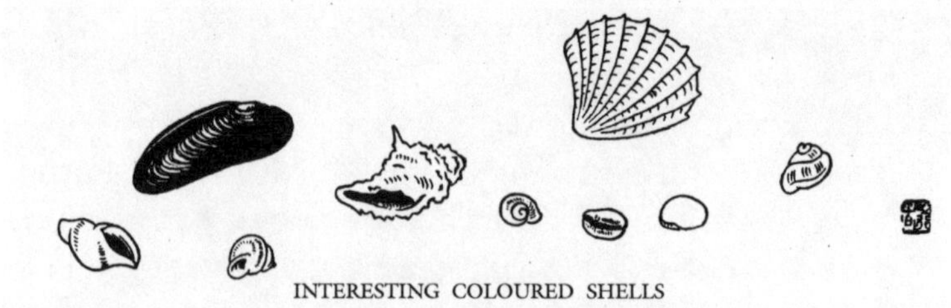

INTERESTING COLOURED SHELLS

Presently I moved away in the same direction as the boys had gone. There were a number of interesting coloured shells lying about. I know nothing about shells myself, but these probably provide a fascinating subject of study for some. I could recognise such common shells as the periwinkle and the dog-whelk, and without intentionally imitating the boys I stooped and picked one up. It was large, with a rough but a distinctive surface pattern. I thought that this and other shells might make useful motifs for designs. There came to my mind the words by D. G. Rossetti:

> Gather a shell from the strewn beach
> And listen at its lips; they sigh
> The same desire and mystery,
> The echo of the whole sea's speech.

I tried in vain to remember any lines by old Chinese poets on the subject, but, as I have said before, we Chinese have little knowledge of the sea, and I doubt whether any of our forefathers ever tried to pick up a shell on the seashore. I therefore composed a little poem of my own:

> Sea and sky fuse without
> trace,
> The rolling waves pursue
> each other.
> Amid all activities I'm alone
> at ease,
> Bending down to pick up a
> shell!

海天渺無角
層浪爭追逐
萬幻我獨閑
折腰拾蚌殼

海灘漫步 啞

I have never considered myself much of a poet, and when my Chinese verses are translated into English I realise that they are apt to sound not very poetical.

From shells my thoughts turned to the scene on the seashore of Hainan Island which I had known twenty-three years before. I was staying with some friends who taught in a public school there. The school was housed in a former German Consulate which had been given back to China after the First World War. It was situated near the seashore and had a large garden with palm trees, coconuts and a small banana grove. It was summer when I went there—but indeed it is always summer on Hainan, for the island lies off the most southerly point of China, near the tropical zone. Every day was fine, all around was green and the sea was calm. The sky was cloudless. None of us wore more clothes than was absolutely necessary. But in the early morning the air was beautifully cool and clear, and almost every morning I took a walk along the seashore to enjoy it, before the heat of the day. It was particularly delightful after the heat of the night.

Sometimes my friend came with me and we talked and walked, gazing around meanwhile. It was amusing to watch the transparent humps of the cuttle-fish slowly revolving in the water near the shore. My friend once struck at one with a small stick and it soon disappeared. Presumably the black liquid which assists its escape is ejected by the fish's bladder. Truly Nature devises wonderful means of protecting her beloved creatures! Another creature that delighted me was a small sea-crab. The tide was very low in the early morning and there was always a large expanse of sand exposed, on which were to be seen a great many of these small crabs apparently also enjoying the early morning air. Each of them had one big claw and a small one instead of two of the same size. When they were stationary the big claw stuck up in the air. No two stood close together. From a distance they looked like a well-disciplined troop on parade. They seemed to possess extraordinarily long sight, for while we were still a good way from them they disappeared as if by magic, leaving in the sand a large number of small holes which were said to be the homes of the crabs. Each crab has its own hole, from which it never strays far, and no one crab may go into the hole of another. If one tries to do so, it is prevented by the owner of the hole. My friend proved this by putting a stick in one of the holes, causing the crab to whom it belonged to try in vain to get into another. Unfortunately, students later tried this trick on a large scale with the object of catching crabs to eat.

SMALL SEA CRABS ON HAINAN ISLAND

Hainan is a large island off the coast of South China and has been a part of China since the Han Dynasty. The well-known Sung poet, Su Tung-p'o, was once governor of it, and evidence of his activities is still visible. The island is rich in natural resources. After my visit I wrote an article about them which was published in the Chinese magazine *Tung-Fang*.

I soon returned to the Promenade. There were a good few people about now, but not so many as one might expect to see during the summer holidays. Perhaps it was due to wartime restrictions, or maybe it was not yet the holiday season. Anyway it was no concern of mine. I went on my way. Two youngsters were running down the sands in the direction from which I had come; someone had led a donkey on to the beach. I did not go back to see what was going to happen.

To my surprise I presently ran into Mr. Edward Ross, with whom I had had tea only three days before. He is a retired judge from India and lives at Regent Terrace near Calton Hill. I had been introduced to him by our mutual friend D. P. Heatley. After tea he had taken me to see the Regent Gardens at the back of his house, and also the many beautiful houses in Regent Terrace and Royal Terrace which are built in eighteenth-century French or Italian style. I thought then that there must be many beautiful residential districts in Edinburgh and hoped that I should find opportunities of visiting them. Now Mr. Ross greeted me by saying how good it was that I was able to take a walk on Portobello Promenade in the sunshine, since it was one of the many beauty-spots of Edinburgh. We agreed that the sea air was particularly healthy and bracing. Then we went on our different ways. Mr. Ross carried an umbrella. I admired the cautiousness of his true Edinburgh nature. I was also glad to see that one could carry an umbrella when walking beside the sea.

I had now come to a part of the Promenade where there were no more houses on my left, but instead a large open space on which a number of rusty articles were lying about and which was enclosed by a low iron fence. As I rested for a while I could see the dark blue shape of Arthur's Seat rising above many hidden buildings in the distance. I thought to myself that the Scots were quite right. From this angle Arthur's Seat looked exactly like a lion, sitting there calmly and majestically. This impression must first have been noted from a ship in the Firth of Forth, and I wondered who had been the first person to land in this part of Scotland and who from a ship in the Firth of Forth first noticed that Arthur's Seat looked like a lion. I doubted whether any Scot could tell me this, even though they are well acquainted with the history of their beloved country. It must be a wonderfully interesting sight to see Arthur's Seat and Edinburgh Castle from a ship in the Firth, and I felt I would like to board one at once. But there was no ship in sight.

Scanning the surface of the sea I suddenly noticed the island of Inchkeith, which I had seen before from Calton Hill. It looked bigger than it had before and less mysterious. I thought how strange it was that my feeling towards one object could change so much and wondered why one is so cocksure of one's own opinion. The clouds were moving fast over the little island, and it seemed to be playing hide-and-seek with me, for sometimes it showed up clearly in the bright sunshine while at others it was lost in the darkness as a heavy cloud moved across the sun—no, not completely lost, for even when the clouds were overhead I could see the small white dots which were seagulls hovering over the island. These did not show up so plainly when the island was in the sun. Suddenly a poem about a lonely island, written by Han Yu, the renowned Confucianist of the T'ang Dynasty, came into my mind:

> In the morning they flutter round the south of the lonely island;
> In the evening they play at the north of the lonely island.
> Therefore the birds of this lonely island
> Know you very well.

I wondered if Inchkeith was privately owned or had been fortified and declared a prohibited area. The latter seemed quite probable. As far as I could make out there was a building with a tower near the highest part of the island. It looked like a big ship with the tower as her funnel, which had been there for thousands of years and would still be there for thousands of years to come. She had been battered by all kinds of weather and been a witness of all Scotland's history since the days of Malcolm Canmore, if not before. I have found this island much less talked about than Arthur's Seat or Edinburgh Castle. There might be some historical events attached to it, but I do not know of them and it does not matter whether I do or not. Nevertheless how true it is that man, and only man, can make things and places great and famous, never the other way round.

Why do so many human beings attach such importance to the place or nation to which they belong? I think nationalism is the stumbling-block in the way of the promotion of world brotherhood. After all, some places may be considered fortunate to be connected with particular historical events and personages; of others the reverse is true. There must still be many places waiting to achieve fame by being connected with some future historical events.

The scudding clouds which changed the colour of the sea from silvery blue to dark blue altered the appearance of Inchkeith too. At one moment it was cloaked in greyish velvet and veiled with a heavy haze, then changed to purplish when it lay full in the sun's focus, and to dark green when the sun was covered. The island also seemed to change its position from time to time. It looked further away from me in the haze than when it was shadowed.

Presently it grew darker as more and more black clouds filled the sky. I wondered where they had all come from, a question I had often asked myself before without ever finding the answer. Soon there was no trace of blue left in the sky; the island almost disappeared in the darkness, and it seemed as though candles were needed to illumine the scene. And, to my surprise, what seemed like a great many candles were being lit up, though the light was whiter and more flickering than normal candle-light. On second thoughts they looked like a cloud of great snow-flakes coming down fast and being blown in all directions—but it was June and there was no wind. The white objects were, in fact, a large cluster of seagulls soaring and circling above the sea near the edge of the shore. They had been there all the time, but I had not noticed them while my attention had been concentrated on the island of Inchkeith. Now I saw them clearly before me. Their brilliant flapping wings looked whiter and more distinct against the black background. One could even notice the degree of difference in whiteness between them and the white-caps of the waves. Some of them were resting on the water, others were hovering above, flapping their wings as if to fan away the thick black clouds; others were lazily circling overhead, occasionally swooping earthwards. A few went right out to sea as far as my eyes could see. Though since I came to live in Britain I have come to love watching the movements of seagulls, I have never known them more interesting than on this occasion. How wonderful that the sky should have darkened in this fashion to reveal this beauty to me!

I wondered why Nature had not given seagulls a camouflaging colour as she did to other creatures. The gulls are neither the colour of the sea nor of the sand. They might be said to look like the white-caps of the waves. But wherever they are, they expose themselves without any sign of fear. Are they, in fact, perfectly secure from danger of attack from any other animal, even from the most cunning of all, man, who seeks to devise means of satisfying his desire for money and food? It is commonly recognised that seagulls are true friends and guides to fishermen. Whenever there are gulls about, the fishermen know they will have a good catch, and so they protect them. Being more or less confined to the sea, seagulls are supposed to do no harm to man, and if they do come inland they are seen following the ploughman in order to pick up insects, which is presumably useful work. Furthermore, as their flesh is coarse and tough they escape being served as a delicacy on the dinner-table...

One evening I was asked to dine with two friends at The Aperitif in Frederick Street, near Princes Street. It was a very comfortable restaurant, decorated, like so many fashionable little Continental places, with modern figure designs on the walls. When the menu was placed before me I spotted seagulls' eggs as one of the choices for the first course. With instinctive curiosity I ordered it right away, and so did my two friends. There were two eggs on each plate, boiled hard. They were about half the size of a good hen's egg and bluish-grey in colour. They showed up well in the midst of the green lettuce and juicy red slices of tomato, and the dish looked most appetising. They tasted good with a little salt and pepper, but my companions seasoned them with French mustard. I had previously tasted pigeons' eggs, the white of which becomes transparent after boiling, but it was a new experience to eat gulls' eggs. Indeed, though I had seen so many seagulls in the British Isles, the thought of eating their eggs had never occurred to me. They seemed to me as good if not better than hens' eggs, and this not only because, owing to the wartime shortage, I had not had many hens' eggs recently.

I asked my companions, who were both citizens of Edinburgh, whether gulls' eggs were easy to buy in their part of the world and whether they could not be used to offset the shortage of hens' eggs, as there must be plenty of them in the British Isles. The reply I got was that gulls' eggs have always been regarded as a delicacy, and that as gulls lay only a few eggs their transport from one place to another was prohibited. This did not prevent my becoming still more interested in eating them. Then I asked whether gulls could not have been used to supplement the scarcity of poultry, but received the same reply as in connection with the eggs. However, I remember reading somewhere that the young birds of the peewit gull or black-cap and of the red-legged gull were thought by some to be good eating. The following passage occurs in Buffon's *Natural History:*

> Most of the kind (the gulls) are fishy tasted, with black stringy flesh: and of these, the poor inhabitants of our northern islands make their wretched banquets. They have been long used to no other food; and even salted gull can be relished by those who know no better. The gull, the petrel, the tern, have all nearly the same habits, the same nature, and are caught in the same manner; that is, at the most imminent risk, and with loss of many lives in the course of a season… Those who have been upon our coasts know that there are

two different kinds of shores; that which slopes towards the water with a gentle declivity, and that which slopes towards the water and appears as a bulwark to repel the force of the invading deep. It is to such shores as these that the vast variety of seafowl resort, and in the cavities of these rocks they breed in safety. Of the tremendous sublimity of these elevations it is not easy to form an idea... To ponder on the terrors of falling to the bottom, where the waves, that swell like mountains, are scarcely seen to curl on the surface, and the roar of the ocean appears softer than the murmur of a brook!... Yet even here these animals are not in perfect security from the arts and activity of man. Want, which is the great spring of human exertion, can force the cottager to tempt the most formidable dangers, and to put forth an endeavour almost beyond the force of man. When the precipice is to be assailed from below, the fowlers furnish themselves with poles of five or six ells in length, with a hook at the end, and fixing one of these poles in the girdle of the person who is to ascend, his companions, in a boat, or on a projection of the cliff, assist his progress till he procures a firm footing. When this is accomplished, he draws the others up with a rope, and another man is forwarded again by means of the pole to a higher station. Frequently the person who is in the highest situation holds another man suspended by a rope, and directs his course to the place where the birds have placed their nests. It unfortunately too often happens that the man who holds the rope has not a footing sufficiently secure, and in that case both of them inevitably perish. Some precipices are so abrupt that they are not by any means to be ascended from below. In this case a rope is provided of eighty or a hundred fathoms long, which one of the fowlers fastens to his waist, and between his legs, in such a manner as to support him in a sitting posture. The rope is held by five or six persons on the top, and it slides upon a piece wood, which is laid so as to project beyond the

> precipice. By means of this apparatus, the man is gradually let down and he attacks the habitations of the feathered race with the most sanguinary success. This operation is, however, not without its dangers. By the descent and friction of the rope the loose stones are furiously hurled down on every side... the festivity of the evening, among these poor and desperate adventurers, generally compensates for the fatigues and dangers of the day.

Want is the mainspring of human exertion! Hunger will drive man to every imaginable and unimaginable effort. From the above description it is clear why there are no seagulls' eggs for sale; furthermore, coastal defences in war prevent the performance of such feats. But should gulls' eggs and flesh prove to be profitable, money might become another strong motive for such exertion.

In China we are known to be bird's-nest eaters. 'Bird's nest (not an agreeable name for a dish)', I wrote in *A Chinese Childhood*, 'is the gelatinous nest of a species of swift or swallow *(Collocalia evirotris)* found on the sea-coast of Fukien, or imported from India. The birds seem to make their nests out of a kind of seaweed or Gelidium. It is a very expensive dish and one which, characteristically, is regarded as a physic for the sick, upon whom it is disputed to have a tonic and invigorating effect.' It is in great demand by those who can afford tonics. To obtain this gelatinous nest is an even harder task than that just described, because it is not found in cavities on the tops of cliffs but on steep cliff-sides. Countless lives have been lost and are still being lost in this adventure along the coasts of Asia. If gulls' eggs and flesh had more of the tonic and health-giving properties of our 'bird's-nests', I can imagine that some scientific method might have been devised for collecting them, thus saving human lives. Nature, however, has saved the gull from extermination by making its flesh unpalatable, though some humans may still risk their lives in an effort to obtain some...

I was aroused from my thoughts by the dark clouds' sudden lifting. I laughed as I realised what effect wartime food problems had had on my mind. The sky was clear again and I could see Inchkeith. The colour of the sea seemed more changeable than ever. But my eyes would not leave the gulls. They are undoubtedly the most interesting birds in the winged kingdom to watch. I love to watch any kind of bird in flight, the graceful heron, the stately swan, the watchful hawk, the darting sparrow, the wheeling swallow, the whirring humming-bird. But none of these displays more indifference to man or such triumphant flight as the seagull. Seagulls are birds of freedom. A French writer, M. de Quatrefages, wrote:

> I saw them describe a thousand curves in the air, then plunge between two waves and reappear with a fish. Flying most swiftly when following the wind, most slowly when facing it, they always flew with the same ease and with no more effort than in the calmest weather. Even when the billows leapt up like cataracts in reverse, as high as the platform of Notre Dame, their spray higher than Montmartre, the gulls appeared unmoved.[1]

How can we mortal men match this philosophy? No wonder that the seagulls visiting St. James's Park screech incessantly at the small-mindedness of those Londoners who boast of the height of Big Ben. Seagulls are the masters of space. They ought to be watched at sea as I was watching them now.

I started to walk along the Promenade again. Walking slowly, I noticed that more seagulls were resting on the wide expanse of sand than flying. Their white feathers showed up clearly in the sun, and at first sight they seemed to be occupying fixed positions, each at a certain distance from the next. Then I saw that they were not standing still, but constantly changing position. Also they had not all the same

1 From *The Birds,* by Jules Michelet, p. 103

white feathers, but some had grey-brown or blackish ones, perhaps in about equal numbers. From their movements they looked more like draughtsmen on a board than birds—just as though a game were being played by two invisible heavenly figures. As there were so many seagulls, perhaps they might be correctly likened to a game of Chinese chess, Wei-chi or *Siege*, in which each player has one hundred and eighty pieces. I used often to play this game when I lived in China, and felt I wanted to be a spectator of this one, so got down on to the sand again. But as soon as I approached the gulls it was as if the chess-board had been overthrown and all the pieces sent flying. Evidently I was an unwanted intruder! At the same time a loud scolding from the gulls rang in my ears. I could stay no longer.

The Promenade had come to an end, nor was it possible to walk further along the sands, but crossing a railway bridge I walked on in the same direction along a narrow path with railings on both sides. I then caught a tram and got down near Newhaven. Though I could not see much of the place, I could smell wine and fish. I wanted to see some Newhaven fishwives in their native costume, but did not know where to look. I remembered a story in the *Evening Dispatch:* 'Two Newhaven fisherwomen wearing their gala dress were seated in an Edinburgh tramcar. Two English soldiers were obviously puzzled. They could make nothing of the scraps of conversation between the women as they sat busily clicking their knitting needles, and ultimately decided that, as the language sounded "a bit like Greek", the women must be from the Balkans!' If the English soldiers could not make out where the Newhaven fishwives came from, it was quite likely I would think they came from India! But what would this matter. I got on another tram for Granton. Through the windows I caught glimpses of the sea. The terminus was at Granton Square near the foot of a small hill, on which were many dwelling-houses which appeared to have been only recently built. In a few years' time when the young trees have grown, Granton should be a pleasant summer resort. As I returned to Edinburgh on the top of a bus, I got the view of Calton Hill, with Arthur's Seat rising behind it, from a different angle. It was interesting to see how the scene gradually came nearer to me, as though I were sitting in a cinema. However, on the whole return journey I was occupied with the thought that for once on my travels I had been an unwanted intruder. But in spite of this, I had thoroughly enjoyed my day beside the sea at Portobello.

XVI

Immediate Comprehension

'Our life', said Chuangtse, one of China's great thinkers, 'is limited, but knowledge is limitless. To pursue the limitless with the limited is hopeless; and to assume that one *does* know is fatal.' As I too am unable to pursue the limitless with the limited I am always happy to be with those of my fellow-creatures who are similarly restricted, namely the animals. The Edinburgh Zoo near Corstorphine has been a sanctuary to me on many occasions.

Sometimes I hear people say that they do not care for Zoos because they do not like to see animals in cages looking miserable. Theoretically I am in complete agreement with them; but the point is really a quibble. Are not we human beings meat-eaters? Has not each of us caused suffering to some animal in one way or another in our time, even though we may not actually have seen it suffer? It is easy to express vehement opinions, but it is sometimes difficult to behave consistently with such opinions. Confucius tried to solve this problem by saying that a gentleman would keep away from the kitchen. But unfortunately not all of us are gentlemen! When Bernard Shaw was ill and was urged by his doctors to eat meat, he remarked, 'Death is better than cannibalism.

My will contains directions for my funeral, which will be followed not by mourning coaches, but by herds of oxen, sheep, swine, flocks of poultry and a small travelling aquarium of live fish, all wearing white scarves in honour of the man who perished rather than eat his fellow-creatures.' Who but G. B. S. could have said that at such a moment?

Probably only the Banians, an Indian race who eat nothing which gives life, can maintain consistently that they disapprove of Zoos. A Banian would not even kill a snake which had bitten him! The Banians throw rice and beans into their rivers and lakes to feed the fishes, and give all kinds of grain to the birds and insects. If they meet a hunter or a fisherman, they try to persuade him to change his occupation. Should their persuasion prove of no avail, they offer to buy his gun or nets. If this effort, too, is fruitless, they stir up the waters to make the fish swim away and try to frighten off the birds with loud cries. It is said that there is at Surat a Banian hospital for animals of all kinds, which includes a ward for rats, mice and all kinds of vermin. However, as I am not a Banian, I do not mind going to the Zoo from time to time. As a matter of fact, no one in charge of Zoological Gardens likes to see the exhibits looking miserable and new ways of making the animals happy are constantly being sought.

George Eliot once wrote: 'Animals are such agreeable friends—they ask no questions, they pass no criticisms.' This is very true. But surely it is a little selfish to make friends of animals simply because they have these qualities. I think that I have immediate comprehension from the behaviour of the animals of what they have to say.

I first visited the Edinburgh Zoo on a September morning in 1943. Immediately I entered it I could see that it lay on the slope of a hill, and was thus better situated than the London Zoo and rather like a small-scale Whipsnade. The first creatures I saw were two polar bears, one lying in the water and the other rolling his head continuously from side to side as if to say 'Oh! So hot, Oh! So hot!' I stood watching him for a while, wondering whether he had adapted himself to the Edinburgh climate or not, and whether he might not now find the Arctic regions a little too cold for him. Near the polar bear enclosure was a group of penguins, the common kind with a black half-circle on the chest like a necklace. They were all standing close together. There was no formal pool to enable them to show off their swift underwater movements as there is in the London Zoo. Nor did I see any king penguins among them. To me the king penguin always suggests a dignified elderly peer in evening dress. Perhaps there are no king penguins in the Edinburgh Zoo because there is no House of Lords in Edinburgh to provide material for comparison!

Next I looked at a grey seal, which was stretched out on a rock in the middle of a little pool. It was enjoying the sunshine and looked completely at ease. Its fur was greyish-yellow, with brownish-black spots. Previously in other Zoos and at circuses I had only seen black-brown or brown seals. As they are usually moving about very swiftly either under the water or on land, I had seldom been able to have as close a look at one as on this occasion.

I enjoyed watching it lie so comfortably with its belly pressed to the rock. Occasionally it moved its head a little to one side, though its eyes remained shut. Then it turned over on to its back, stretched its neck and yawned. Had it not been for its double-pointed tail I would have taken it for a stout Edinburgh citizen relaxing after a few glasses of Younger's ale or Black and White whisky.

I am told that there is a traditional respect for the seal among the inhabitants of the Irish coast, and that Scottish fishermen regard the killing of a seal as unlucky. This kind of superstition serves Nature's purpose well. Apart from what I have seen for myself of the intelligence of seals in playing with balls and playing tunes on musical instruments at circuses, I have also read that it is capable of showing marked affection to its human friends when it is tamed and domesticated. In an old issue of the *Field* magazine a writer told how he was given a young seal by some fishermen and took it home. After a few weeks it followed him about, took food from his hand and recognised him at once from a distance. It was very fond of heat and would lie for hours in front of the kitchen fire just like a dog. One severe and stormy winter, when fish could not be obtained, it learned to drink milk. Eventually the writer decided to put the seal back into the sea, but it swam so fast after his boat, crying loudly and pitifully, that he had to take it home again. Another story, in Maxwell's *Wild Sports of the West*, tells of a tamed seal which lived with a family for several years. Though it was repeatedly put back into the sea, it as often returned to the house it loved, even contriving to creep through an open window and make its way to the warm fireside. What interests me in these stories is that a seal, which normally lives most of its life in cold sea-water, appears to possess an innate love of warmth. It would be interesting to know if seals could live permanently on land without ever seeing the sea.

Passing the enclosure containing some Chinese golden pheasants, which provided a feast of colour for my eyes, I found myself among the birds. Their sanctuary was enclosed by a stone wall and one entered through a small gate. In the centre were a great many rose bushes in full bloom. Unfortunately the collection of birds was rather poor, possibly due to wartime conditions. But in a big dovecot I saw a fantail pigeon sticking its chest out so as almost to hide its head. It stood still for a while and then took a few steps while making circular movements with its chest. It made no noise, yet gave the impression of playing to a huge audience. I could not help laughing at it. How often have I not seen similar sights among human beings, though without on those occasions being able to laugh.

I passed on to a large wire-netted house containing rhesus monkeys. Inside were some tree trunks on which they could jump about and climb. There were three baby monkeys, one of which was still so young that it clung to its mother's chest all the time. The other two were very mischievous and playful. They followed the fully grown monkeys about and imitated them, though sometimes they could not grasp the branches tightly enough and fell off. However frightened they may have been, they soon tried to climb back again. Some of them were splashing water from a little earthen bath just like human children. The big monkeys quarrelled the whole time, fighting and screaming. They are so like humans that I can never see them without smiling. Suddenly I heard a noise coming from behind some tall trees. A boy attendant and two women keepers were trying to get a gibbon out of one cage into another, so that they could do some cleaning job. It refused to move until they turned a hose on it, when, since gibbons, unlike rhesus monkeys, have no love for water, it went out at once. As soon as it was out it gave a long high-pitched cry, either of anger or vexation. In China the monkey's cry is considered sad and indicative of a longing for friends or home. Many of our great poets have composed verses about this to symbolise their own feelings. One poem written by the T'ang Emperor Tai Tsung of the eighth century depicts a wonderful scene on an autumn night:

> As the evening mist rose, the distant shore became obscure:
> As the moon went down, half the cliffs darkened.
> What has startled the birds in the mountains?
> Over the nearest peak came the cry of a lonely monkey!

I seemed to hear that cry now, though the setting was very different. As a result of the rapid changes due to mass migration inland during the present war and the improvement of communications in China, the monkeys' cry will no longer be heard along the mountains of the south-west as described in the T'ang poems, so perhaps these will not have the same charm for future generations.

Alongside the rhesus monkeys were a number of big cages for the chimpanzees. One chimpanzee named Philip was given a lighted cigarette by a woman keeper. He took it and put the right end into his mouth like an experienced smoker. He was able to blow the smoke out through his nostrils without making himself cough. No doubt he had smoked before, perhaps every day. I understand that people who have acquired the smoking habit cannot bear to give it up even for a short interval, and I wondered what Philip would do if his woman keeper was not about or had no cigarette to offer him. He would just have to control himself. Another onlooker remarked: 'A beast with human intelligence. Is it not wonderful!' This set me thinking of my fellow-beings trying to kill each other in war: 'A man with beast's intelligence. Is it not horrible!' In some respects, men are no better than beasts. So long as they have enough food to eat and are safe from danger, wild beasts do not kill each other for ideological reason. But…

I went on down a path, both sides of which were lined with trees and bushes. Beyond one low hedge I could see a number of yellow, pink and red flowers, mostly roses. One of the advantages of the Edinburgh Zoo is that I can enjoy not only the animals but also the flowers. In other Zoos too there are flowers to be seen, but only the Edinburgh Zoo seems like a botanical garden. This is due, I think, to its compactness and to its naturally hilly situation. I saw a number of butterflies hovering round the flowers. I have not seen many of these in the British Isles, probably due to the rather cold climate. But these particular ones seemed to be quite happy as they hovered and danced with ever-increasing speed from flower to flower.

As I moved along another bushy lane I tried to remember the details of 'Summoning Butterflies' which I had read in an old Chinese book, *Ku-chin-pi-yuan*. It tells one to collect a number of flower stamens and pistils and, after letting them dry in a cold place for seven days and nights, to mix them

PUBLIC SPEAKERS BY THE SIDE OF THE ROYAL SCOTTISH ACADEMY

with some honey. Thereafter, if one sees butterflies hovering about, one puts a little of this mixture on one's palm, rubs the hands together and raises them with palms outstretched in the direction of the prevailing wind. At this fragrant summons all the butterflies soon gather round. In the old days in China it was an ingenious game for ladies of big families to play in their beautiful and spacious gardens. They had plenty of time then and did not go out much. I am afraid it would not be possible for modern Chinese ladies to play this game as they are now complaining about lack of time as much as their sisters in the West. This little game may sound nonsense to the scientist, but it is a charming idea and certainly indicates the tranquility of life in former times. Nowadays we make use of every minute, but I doubt whether we have gained much. I would rather play with butterflies than dash down the escalator into a London tube.

I would like to design a ballet based on this game of 'Summoning Butterflies'. Science has made possible many innovations in lighting and colours for the modern stage, but it is not yet feasible to have livestock on the stage, though I once saw fantail pigeons there. I think it would be an interesting experiment for a ballerina to put some of the above-mentioned mixture on her palms and see if she could summon butterffies to hover round her while she danced. Perhaps modern scientific methods could produce a better mixture, but the ultimate success of the affair would, of course, rest with the butterflies. This kind of ballet could only be performed in a hot country in summer. Some day, who knows, I may see my fancy realised.

As I loitered along day-dreaming, a boy dashed down from a slope and bumped right into me, rousing me rudely from my thoughts. 'Pardon me, sir', he said, and disappeared in a flash. He was the boy attendant I had seen in the chimpanzees' quarter; I realised that I was still in Edinburgh Zoo. A big stone dropped from the branch of a tall tree and I heard someone running; another stone dropped and again I heard running footsteps. This happened yet a third time, and finally I saw the boy who had just bumped into me running quickly towards me with his hands over his ears. I asked him what he was doing. He pointed to a tree in the distance, and said that there was a big wasps' nest in it and that the wasps had stung him badly. 'What about me and the other people walking here?' I queried. The boy laughed and said that the wasps would only sting him who had disturbed their nest but would do no harm to me or others. I could not help laughing, for I was amused to think that wasps could distinguish between friends and enemies.

I next found myself in a small house with a number of cages on either side, some containing mice and rabbits and the rest monkeys. A baby baboon looking very lonely and sad was in a small cage all by himself. I noticed another monkey sitting right at the top of its cage, with its back to me. A small notice told me that this was Rosie, a stump-tailed monkey from S.E. Asia. I thought that it might have come from China or Japan. It was some time before I got a glimpse of its face, and then I nearly cried out in surprise for it was red all over and looked just as though the contents of a rouge-box had been used on it, if you can imagine such a thing. Rosie was certainly a good name for this particular monkey. One of Nature's jokes!

Next I watched two young, brownish-grey bears playing and wrestling together in their cage, like a couple of children. Sometimes they stood on their hind-legs, moving their fore-paws like boxers. Sometimes they rolled over and over on the ground, and sometimes one climbed on top of the other and fell off flat when the other gave himself a sudden

ROSIE

shake. They played continuously and caused much laughter among the many people looking at them. An elderly lady with a Rubens figure simply could not stop giggling and kept saying, 'Oh, funny beers, oh, funny beers!' I thought that she had been drinking, but later realised that the Scots pronounce 'bear' beer. In any case these two playful bears produced the same effect on this elderly lady as a glass of beer.

Though Edinburgh Zoo must have lost some exhibits owing to the war, there remained quite a lot for me to see. I had already seen the small aquarium, where a fish called Hi Goi was new to me. I thought it must be a Scottish fish with such a name, but no one could enlighten me on this point. Now I had a good look at a group of lion cubs and also inspected the llamas, ponies, deer and wallabies.

As I was climbing up one of the slopes, a soldier with a black moustache called out, 'Have you got any matches, sonny?' When I answered that I was not a smoker, he and his family all laughed and he said 'Bad luck'. I wondered why he called me 'sonny'. Perhaps my bushy black hair had given him an impression of youthfulness from a distance. I remember that once when I was walking along a mountain path, near Fort William, a young Highland boy with whom I entered into conversation could not believe that I was more than forty years old, as my hair was still so black. Alas, I have grown a few grey hairs since I left my own country! Modern scientists are seeking means to enable human beings to live two hundred and fifty years. By these standards I am indeed a mere youngster. Perhaps that is why I have always enjoyed being with animals and have even felt a kind of kinship with them.

I now approached the houses of the tigers and lions. Near the tiger house I noticed with interest a small Himalayan bear, only a little bigger than a puma, jet black in colour with a white chest. It was the smallest bear I had ever seen. The arrangement of the tiger house in Edinburgh Zoo is admirable.

There is a dark shady passage in front. The house itself contains shrubs amid grasses and many small red and yellow wild flowers, and against this natural background the tawny, black-striped coats of Rajah and Ranee stood out vividly. One of them was standing motionless on a rock, looking majestically in my direction, while the other climbed slowly up and down as if performing some exercise, making a series of ideal subjects for an artist. My own fingers were itching to paint. The tiger is one of my favourite subjects, partly because of its beautiful colouring and partly because of its expression at once docile and courageous. Its ferocity, when frightened or hungry, I do not care to think about; but why should I? The behaviour of human beings when suffering from fear and hunger is hardly less unpleasant.

I suddenly recalled a Chinese fairy-story about a tiger. It is said that in the year Tien-pao of the T'ang Dynasty a court flute-master escaped from the palace after a rebellion, and hid himself in a monastery on the Chung-nan mountain. One clear moonlit night he felt homesick for the palace and began to play his bamboo flute. He was a renowned flautist and his melody seemed to float over the whole mountainside. Suddenly a man in white with a tiger head came into the monastery courtyard. The flute-master trembled with fear and nearly fell off the stone steps on which he was sitting. The tiger-head man said that the tune was very good and asked him to play again. So the flautist continued to play until the tiger-head man fell asleep and snored loudly. Stealthily the musician crept out and climbed up on to the branch of a tall tree, where the thick foliage would hide him. Presently the tiger-head man woke up and found the flute-master gone. 'What a pity not to have eaten him earlier!' he said with a sigh; 'now he has run away.' Thereupon he gave a long whistle and a number of tigers came and bowed to him. He ordered them to run in all directions in search of the flute-master. They did not find him until the moon lit up the tall tree in which he was hiding. Then all the tigers laughed and said the master must be an immortal who could come and go like clouds and lightning; but although he was, in fact, a mere mortal they could not catch him, not even the tiger-head man himself, though they all jumped up at the tree until they were exhausted. Finally they went away, and at dawn the flute-master came down from the tree. It was fortunate for him that tigers cannot climb.

The arrangement of the Edinburgh lion house also seemed to me very attractive. Though the Zoo is finely situated on a slope, a perceptive eye was needed to make the most of this natural advantage. I must congratulate whoever designed the houses for the lions and tigers. At the top of an ascending footpath was a sort of cave where six young lion cubs were playing among very naturally arranged rocks. There was a barrier to prevent the cubs escaping, but I could see them enjoying chasing one another as well as if there had been no barrier at all. There was a small waterfall running down the rocks and a few wild flowers dotted here and there which gave an added beauty to the scene. All Zoo animals should, I think, be kept in such natural surroundings. Then no one could say that they do not like to see animals in cages. The next lion house had a number of lions in separate cages on either side. There was a cave in the middle of this house too, and in it three very young cubs were rolling on top of one another. An opening led from this into an inner cave, where the mother of the cubs, Topsy, was lying drowsily. Presently she got up and walked into the main part of the cave, whereupon the three little cubs became more playful than ever. One bit its mother's tail and another tried to pull her whiskers with its fore-paw. Topsy was very patient and showed no annoyance with her children. Her every gesture showed her care and tenderness for them. As I considered the possibility of painting the lioness and her cubs, I remembered reading two letters about Landseer's Lions in *The Times* one day.

Mr. G. A. Anson wrote:

Landseer's lions have from time to time produced quite a lot of speculative correspondence—speculative, because written without knowledge of the actual facts. A correspondent in your issue of today makes the suggestion that Landseer's drawing was made from a dead lion, and that his 'error' (*i.e.*, an alleged mistake in drawing a lion with his fore-legs out in front) was due to his model not being a living beast. But Landseer made no mistake—he drew the animal which he saw, and no one has ever been more exact in reproducing animals from life.

During the time that Sir Edwin was engaged in preparing his drawings for the lions, my grandmother, the Duchess of Abercorn, went to see Landseer (who was a personal friend) at his home in St. John's Wood. She was shown into the garden, where she found him sketching a huge lion which was lying on the lawn in front of him at complete liberty, and in the exact attitude of the 'Landseer Lion'. My grandmother was slightly nervous, but Sir Edwin said: 'Never mind, dearie, he won't hurt you.'

Mr. H. P. Betts wrote:

As one of the few whose memory goes back so far, may I supply some facts? Sir Edwin Landseer was staying with my father, for whom he painted his picture 'Morning in Braemar', at Preston Hall, when he received a letter telling him that the old lion at the Zoo was dead. He turned to my mother and said, 'The King of Beasts is dead and I must be off'. When we children, with whom Sir Edwin was a great favourite, asked why he had gone, we were told that a question of anatomy was puzzling him and he wished to examine the skeleton. The lions are not at rest, but erect, ready to rise, with paws stretched out straight to grip the soil. No one who knows what an accurate observer Sir Edwin was can think of him as making sketches from a dead beast propped up by its keeper.

These letters reveal to me an attitude to works of art frequently adopted by Westerners. I sincerely hope Sir Edwin Landseer was not merely aiming at an accurate likeness when he modelled his lions. It should be the artist's aim to reveal the spirit and inner significance of his subject. Anatomical accuracy and physical likeness should not be neglected, but art cannot be analysed through a microscope or any other scientific device.

I decided to shake off my thoughts by climbing to the top of the nearest hill, for it is another advantage of Edinburgh Zoo that one can easily get right away from all the animals if one wants to. I walked on into a pine grove. Above my head the winds tossed the clusters of pine needles together, producing a sound like the ebb and flow of waves. I had gone up there to get away from noises, but this was an agreeable sound and I listened to it attentively. It seemed to intensify the stillness of the surroundings. I did not wish to say anything, nor to trouble myself with unnecessary thought. A minute passed in this tranquility acted like a shower of rain on the dry soil of my mind. Then I heard another sound, similar to that made by the wind-blown pines, but stronger. Yet even this did not disturb the prevailing peacefulness: it was the sound of water striking against the rocky cliff on which I was standing. I had not realised that there was a deep green pool far below. White curls of foam formed and broke on the surface of the water. A few seagulls wheeled up and down, as if they were conducting an orchestra of the waves and the pines. I sat down on a rock with my back against the trunk of a pine, looking towards Edinburgh Castle and Calton Hill in the distance. They were shrouded in summer haze, yet were unmistakable. None of these things—sea, cliff, pines or seagulls—showed any sign of recognition of my presence. They had seen kings, queens, princes, noblemen, rich men and poor men—all insignificant by comparison with themselves. Why should they bother about me?

I composed a poem to make an enjoyable conclusion to my day:

As I sit on the rocky cliff,
The pine-scented wind refreshes my mind.
Then I stand to look down at the huge sea-pool;
How deep is the blue-green water!
Where will my life be anchored?
Floating and sinking like the water birds is the way for me.
There is a beginning and an end for all creatures;
Hustle and bustle make no difference to ancient or modern.
I enjoy the moment, forgetting the world for a while,
And the white clouds watch me humming.

小坐崖石上松風清我心
俯觀臨巨壑碧海何其深
吾生將焉寄浮沉若水禽
萬物有終始擾擾無古今
樂此暫忘世白雲聽我吟

登愛丁堡動物園後山 吟

xvii

Eventful Reflection

At no one place in Edinburgh did I spend more time than in a field beside Jeanie Deans' Cottage. Over and over again I went there to look at the view of Salisbury Crags and Arthur's Seat. To me it was like a Chinese painting on a horizontal scroll by one of the great Sung masters. When it was a fine clear day and there were a few figures dotted about, the scene seemed to be in the style of Li Chao-tao; while in mist and heavy fog it was undoubtedly in the style of Hsia Kuei or Ma Yuan. As it is almost always shrouded in mist it resembles a monochrome rather than a painting in colours. Anyone who cannot understand Chinese painting, particularly the artists' fondness for Chinese black ink, would here be helped towards an understanding of it.

One morning I wanted to have a look at Craigmillar Castle, but instead of going there by bus, I decided to walk by way of Duddingston Loch. And almost unconsciously I found myself again in the field beside Jeanie Deans' Cottage. Everything was shrouded in thick fog; the Cottage seemed farther away than usual. Then I noticed something struggling to pierce the mists, and in a moment Arthur's Seat came into view, apparently suspended in space. On this occasion I could see its generally accepted resemblance to a lion's head rather than to that of an elephant, which is how it usually looks to me. It appeared so aloof and solitary that at first it seemed more like a dream than reality. Gradually other rocks and ridges emerged out of the mist, their sizes and shapes all altered by the fog. Near the ground it was still very thick and the little path between the gap on the hillside and Salisbury Crags was not yet visible. I watched a passer-by go down this path, growing fainter and fainter and finally vanishing. As my glance strayed from Arthur's Seat to Salisbury Crags I noticed beneath them some small round moving objects which looked like a group of young children playing under cover of a big sheet. When the fog cleared I saw they were sheep. Having feasted my eyes for a time I turned towards Queen's Drive.

On my way I thought about photographic perspective and of perspective in Chinese landscape paintings. Many art critics in the West think either that there is no perspective at all in Chinese pictorial art or else that our way of showing it is most peculiar. But the eye does not reflect a view in exactly the same way as the lens of a camera. No camera reproduces adequately a misty or foggy scene. The distant mountain images, faintly visible to the eye, are not reproduced in a photograph. Moreover, in a photograph high mountain ranges in the background may appear to be below the level of the mountains in the foreground, which is not supported by the evidence of the eyes. The Chinese method of painting tries to represent the landscape as it appears to the eye. Our ideas of perspective are perhaps not scientific, as we often purposely exaggerate a little by elevating distant objects and showing the effect of a scene as it would appear from somewhere higher up than the artist in fact is. I hope art critics may come to have a look at Arthur's Seat and Salisbury Crags veiled in morning mist.

There was a public seat on the hilltop at the beginning of Queen's Drive and I sat down for a while. The whole of

Edinburgh lay before me, but only some of its landmarks were visible through the mist. Two lines of a poem written by a Sung poet Kuo Chang-ken came to my mind:

> The morning mist has suddenly vanished only to
> reappear;
> The spring mountains seem now near, now distant.

I felt I wanted to substitute 'Edinburgh Castle' for 'spring mountains'.

As I went downhill it began to rain. I saw a man chasing a dog with a rabbit in its mouth. We exchanged greetings and he added, 'A wee one. Not worth it.' Involuntarily I replied in the Scottish way, 'Nae ba'', wondering if he was using his little dog to hunt food for his own consumption.

Presently I came to Samson's Ribs, the most rocky part of the hillside, and looked down on Duddingston Loch and its surroundings. As it was raining harder than ever, the view was not very clear. It looked as though there was a small range of hills behind the loch. A scene veiled by a transparent rain-curtain always fascinates me. The rippled surface of the loch indicated that there was a strong wind below, yet the rain was coming straight down. Then a gust caught me in the back. I could hardly stand upright, I seemed to feel the pressure of each minute particle of fog borne along by the wind. I expected at any moment to be thrown into the loch. I could see nothing below me except a few tiny dots which I knew must be the swans on the loch, though where they had come from and where they were going to puzzled me. I felt alone in a blotted-out world and imagined myself to be the reincarnation of some young prince from Scotland's past who must surely at some time have stood and dreamt where I now stood.

I suddenly noticed a solitary figure close by who seemed to have appeared from nowhere. I moved towards it, but the individual paid no heed to my approach, not even looking in my direction. I became curious and thought that he must be looking at something particularly interesting, so I went right up to him. At first neither of us uttered a word, but while I was still trying to find out what he was so interested in, he at last turned to look at me. He wore a weather-beaten hat and had long white hair, a bushy white moustache and beard and rosy cheeks. His expression was solemn and he looked like the personification of the old Scots whom I had seen portrayed in Scottish history-books. I did not know how to respond to his surprised glance, but he eased the tension by addressing me:

'Have you been to this country before?'

'Yes,' I answered.

'Have you been to the Castle?'

'Yes.'

'Have you walked down the Royal Mile?'

'Yes.'

'Have you seen the Heart of Midlothian?'

'Yes.'

'Have you spat on it?'

'No. Why?'

'For luck.'

'Why luck?'

'Have you read about Oliver Cromwell?'

'I know his name, but not much about him.'

'Ah, young man, I tell you.' He lifted his right arm and pointed straight ahead into the fog, 'Round a mile there. Our auld enemy, the English, cannot come directly from the Firth, but...' His words flowed on like running water, with occasional pauses and emphases. They were beyond my understanding and I could not follow him at all, though now and then I distinctly heard the words 'auld enemy'. I stared at him intently, while his eyes, looking in the direction where his fingers were pointing, seemed to fill with tears. He took it for granted that I could follow what he was saying, and I had no chance to ask him why Cromwell had come to Edinburgh.

He expected me to know not only English history but Scottish too. During my stay in England I seem to have come across references to Cromwell everywhere, but this was the first time in Edinburgh. At last the old man paused, but only for a second. Then he went on to say that Sir Walter Scott had actually written *The Heart of Midlothian* in the garden which now belonged to him. Of course I had to be reminded of Scott too! Afterwards he told me what to look out for as I went down the road, particularly stressing that I should go and have a look at Duddingston old Parish Church, from where I could see his garden. I took advantage of this opening to say goodbye to him and continued on my way. As I watched the fog gradually dispersing and the scenery reappearing, my head cleared. I looked back once or twice at the old gentleman before he was lost to my sight. I admired his national pride.

HEART OF MIDLOTHIAN

The Scots are indeed a patriotic race and I have had many experiences like this one. Once I was travelling from Glasgow to Fort William, and in the same compartment with me was a Glasgow man who was going to the same destination for a fishing holiday. He told me that he had been in Shanghai as an engineer for some firm and would like to go there again when the war was over. Naturally I entered into conversation with him, in the course of which I made various references to 'the English'. I meant by this the people from the British Isles as a whole, including the Scots who were living in Shanghai. This is the normal way of referring to them; even Americans would do the same. To my surprise this Glaswegian stopped me, saying seriously, 'Don't keep saying "the English", "the English" while you are up North. If you go beyond Fort William and still call us "the English" the people will kill you.' I remembered various stories about the English and the Scots always being at loggerheads. One which always makes me smile is told by John Duncan in his *The Thistle and The Rose:*

> A stout English visitor to one of the fashionable watering-places on the West Coast some years ago was in the habit of conversing familiarly with Donald Fraser, a character of the place, who took delight in talking boastfully of his great relations, who existed only, the stranger suspected, in the Highlander's own lively imagination. One day, as the Englishman was seated at the door of his lodging, Donald came up driving a big fat boar. 'One of your relations, I suppose, Donald?' exclaimed the visitor, chuckling and nodding his head in the direction of the 'porker'. 'No,' quietly retorted Donald, surveying the proportions of his interlocutor, 'no relation at all, sir, but just an acquaintance, *like yoursel.*'

This simple story tells me a great deal about the characters of some at least of the Scots and the English. Donald might have made the same reply to me if I had jested with him as the stout English visitor did. But somehow I feel he would not have done so, though I cannot explain why, unless it is that, whereas the English sense of humour expects a chuckle, the Scottish one is satisfied with a *passive* smile and in this is very similar to the Chinese. This is perhaps due to the historical background of each country: China has had a troubled history, and as her people have had to adjust themselves to circumstances tolerantly and philosophically, her sense of humour is typified by *passive* smiles. On a smaller scale the history of Scotland has also been troubled, and the Scots have not always got their own way like the English. The English instinctively express their feelings spontaneously. They know that their country is famous for its sense of humour. Some of them, especially the fashionable young highbrows, try to crack jokes in any circumstances and sometimes land themselves in an awkward position, as the stout English visitor did with Donald.

But no matter how sharp the differences between the English and the Scots, they will always unite to resist any danger which might damage their two countries as a whole. Confucius' great disciple, Mencius, said: 'Brothers who may quarrel within the walls of their home, will bind themselves together to drive away any intruder.' But my compatriots of the present day lack this spirit. I salute the Scottish benevolent spirit of brotherhood and wish it could be extended to the whole world so that wars might cease.

I next turned my thoughts to the old man's reference to spitting for luck on the 'Heart of Midlothian' in the middle of Edinburgh's High Street. I do not pretend to know much about the Heart of Midlothian, and would like to find out the origin of this custom. I remembered noticing evidence of spitting there on one or two occasions. Perhaps this area is outside the jurisdiction of the sanitary inspector of Edinburgh. I wondered whether this spitting for luck would long be continued. However, it was pointless to go on asking myself these rhetorical questions.

Presently I reached Duddingston Loch. It was quite small but I could not get to the water's edge. I could see a few swans clustered together in the distance looking like a huge white ball. The surface of the loch was as smooth as a mirror. The tower of the parish church, a low stone wall and some trees were all clearly reflected in it. I could also see in it two little coloured dots moving about near the church tower, and which I was soon able to identify as two figures, one in army uniform and the other in a red jumper, who were walking beside the loch. They were the only human beings I had seen since leaving the old man, and they were too far away to disturb the tranquility of the scene.

I left the hillside and the loch and entered a lane flanked by old houses on both sides. As it was narrow and extremely quiet, my footsteps sounded very clearly. Turning to the right, I saw a small stone gate leading to Duddingston Parish Church. I tried in vain to figure out the position of the old man's garden where he said Sir Walter Scott once sat and wrote *The Heart of Midlothian,* then went on my way without looking into the church. The complete silence, undisturbed by so much as a sparrow hopping about, oppressed me. I peeped into the front gardens of many of the old houses and found them full of flowers. In one of them I saw a small flowering tree in a corner near the main gate. It still had a number of big flowers on the twigs, though they had been badly battered by the recent violent rainstorm. At first sight I took it for a rose tree but the flowers were too big for that, so then the idea occurred to me that it might be a tree peony, a thought which I found very stimulating, for this is a flower much prized by us Chinese. Our great men-of-letters have written endless poems and essays in praise of it and there are a large number of romantic stories about it. It is called Moutan, the *Flower of Prosperity*...

There is a place called Lo-Yang in Honan Province where the tree peony grows at its best for the reason given in the following legend, which I have already related in my book *A Chinese Childhood.*

The Empress Wu Tsai-T'ien of the T'ang Dynasty (A.D. 690–697), who is the only woman to have established herself on the throne as head of the whole Chinese empire, thought there was nothing she could not demand. One winter day she wanted to hold a festival in her Palace Garden and wished all the flowering trees to be in blossom for the occasion. So she ordered the chief eunuch to hang up a board in time garden with the following poem of hers on it:

Tomorrow morning I go to the Palace Garden:
Make haste to tell the Spring!
Flowers must blossom this very night,
Not wait until the dawn wind blows.

The eunuch had to obey, and naturally he and all the Court were greatly worried. He ordered a number of people to beat drums in the garden in the hope of encouraging the flowers to bloom. And next morning they were all in flower, but with one exception—the tree peony! The Empress was furious at this disobedience and ordered that all the tree peonies in the Palace Garden should at once be burned. As the fire was consuming them the peonies suddenly burst into bloom and extinguished the flames. Though the Empress enjoyed this beautiful spectacle very much she still felt greatly displeased with the tree peonies for not obeying her imperial order, so she told her eunuchs to send them all to Lo-Yang, far away from the capital Changan, as a punishment. The tree peonies have flourished there ever since. And to this day in some famous gardens the stems are burnt before blossoming-time, for this is said to make the flowers bigger and finer than usual.

I wondered whether this 'tree peony' had any connection with Lo-Yang, as it must certainly have been of Chinese origin.

I had not seen a tree peony for many years, though I had seen many of the herbal type. The gate of the house was locked, so I could not examine the bush closely. Perhaps this was just as well.

One particularly popular Chinese poem about the peony, by an unknown poet, runs as follows:

A lady plucked a peony flower full of dew-drops like pearls.
Crossing the courtyard, she asked her love smilingly:
'Which is more beautiful, the flower or my face?'
In a teasing mood, her love gave all the praise to the flower.
She answered him with girlish anger
By crushing the flower and tossing it over him.

Everybody can appreciate this little display of human frailty! I looked again at the tree peony and saw that more petals had been blown down, so I moved on.

I walked for a good while, gazing all around me. Two people whom I met a long distance apart each told me it was about a *mile walk* to Craigmillar Castle. Then I looked over a short stone wall and saw Duddingston Loch again with a large number of seagulls resting on it, while a cluster of them was flying above it. Had it not been for the sound of their cry and their flight I might have passed the loch without noticing it. I wanted to have a closer look at the swans but could not find a gate in the wall.

Going on again, I asked yet a third person; I was again told it was *a mile walk* to Craigmillar Castle. I began to compare this *mile walk* with the invariable answer *'a five minutes' walk'* given by any London policeman.

On reaching Peffermill Road, I at last found myself in sight of the Castle. A group of youngsters playing in the middle of a side-road stopped for a moment to stare at me. This road went up to a farm from which a hilly path led up to the Castle. I could not see any way into the grounds, and although I noticed two women and a young girl in front of the farm, they were talking in so animated a fashion that I was reluctant to interrupt their gossip by asking how to get up to the Castle. In any case, I would not have been able to study its architecture as I am no architect. It is said to be the 'only example in Scotland of a family mansion systematically built on the principles of fortification in use during the fifteenth and sixteenth centuries'.

I was feeling quite tired after a good day's walk, so I went through the steading until I reached a place from where I could command a general view of the Castle. I leaned against a wall and supported my head in my hands while I gazed at the scene before me. The sky was very grey, and the distant hills of Arthur's Seat showed up dark blue against it. A thin white vapour rising up from below veiled the jagged outlines of the dwelling-houses scattered about. However, there was as yet no evening mist covering the slopes below the Castle. The grass was all of the same shade of green, as there was no sunshine to provide light and shade. A few cows were still grazing very quietly as if not wanting to disturb the tranquil scene. Their brown-and-white bodies harmonised with the greyish-yellow stones of the Castle and with its ruined roofless tower. Above the Castle one or two seagulls hovered in circles, then flew away and were lost to sight. They intensified rather than disturbed the serenity of the place.

CRAIGMILLAR CASTLE

I reflected on the eventful days of the reigns of James III and Mary Queen of Scots. I had read about their connection with this Castle, though I could not vouch for the authenticity of the tales. James III was considered the King of Peace, who with his over-refined disposition and preference for quiet occupations always feared his two manly and chivalrous brothers, the Dukes of Mar and Albany. So he imprisoned the younger of them, John of Mar, in this Castle for treason, and John never came out alive. As I thought of it, I seemed to see the scene as it was in those bygone days of 1479. The few cows in the field were no longer cows but the fat, colourful prison guards pacing round slowly and soundlessly on their routine duties. The trees cast a dark shadow over the Castle, giving it a sombre appearance. I tried in vain to visualise the appearance of the King's youngest brother and wondered how he had passed his days. Human sorrow does not even spare a handsome prince!

It is said that Craigmillar Castle was the favourite country residence of Mary Queen of Scots. I can well believe it. Neither stately Edinburgh Castle nor luxurious Holyroodhouse could provide solace for the troubled heart of this unhappy young queen. She must have found State affairs tiresome at times. And she did not care much for giving audience to John Knox. What she wanted was an object for her affections. What better place could she find than Craigmillar Castle in which to indulge her love-sick heart? I could see her there now, sitting in her boudoir with her eyebrows knit and her lips pressed very tightly together. In my imagination the cows now became her healthy-looking, barrel-shaped lords-in-waiting, moving restlessly about, seeking ways to please their royal mistress. The seagulls hovering above the Castle became the royal standards blown by the wind. How many times had the young queen come to sit here, to brood over her unhappy fate? Mortal tragedy touched the common folks less than the beautiful queen!

A fresh wind suddenly blew up and I shook my head. Some wild-rose petals from a rambler growing over the wall fluttered to the ground by my feet. Falling petals always mean sadness to a Chinese, and I was no exception on this occasion. I recalled the falling petals of the tree peony which I had seen near Duddingston Parish Church. I should like to quote here a well-known *Song of burying flowers* by a love-stricken young girl Lin Tai-Yu in an outstanding Chinese novel *Hung-Lou-Meng* written during the latter half of the seventeenth century. Almost every young Chinese can recite this beautiful song by heart. The late Professor Herbert A. Giles made a good translation of it in English:

> Flowers fade and fly,
> and flying fill the sky;
> Their bloom departs, their perfume gone,
> yet who stands pitying by?
> And wandering threads of gossamer
> on the summer-house seen,
> And falling catkins lightly dew-steeped
> strike the embroidered screen.
> A girl within the inner rooms,
> I mourn that spring is done,
> A skein of sorrow binds my heart,
> and solace there is none.
> I pass into the garden,
> and I turn to use my hoe,
> Treading o'er fallen glories
> as I lightly come and go.
> There are willow-sprays and flowers of elm,
> and these have scent enow,
> I care not if the peach and plum
> are stripped from every bough.
> The peach tree and the plum tree too
> next year may bloom again,

But next year, in the inner rooms,
  tell me, shall I remain?
By the third moon new fragrant nests
  shall see the light of day,
New swallows flit among the beams,
  each on its thoughtless way.
Next year once more they'll seek their food
  among the painted flowers,
But I may go, and beams may go,
  and with them swallow bowers.
Three hundred days and sixty make
  a year, and therein lurk
Daggers of wind and swords of frost
  to do their cruel work.
How long will last the fair fresh flower
  which bright and brighter glows?
One morn its petals float away,
  but whither no one knows.
Gay blooming buds attract the eye,
  faded they're lost to sight;
Oh, let me sadly bury them
  beside these steps tonight!
Alone, unseen, I seize my hoe,
  with many a bitter tear;
They fall upon the naked stem
  and stains of blood appear.
The night-jar now has ceased to mourn,
  the dawn comes on apace,
I seize my hoe and close the gates,
  leaving the burying place;
But not till sunbeams fleck the wall
  does slumber soothe my care,
The cold rain pattering on the pane
  as I lie shivering there.

You wonder that with flowing tears
  my youthful cheek is wet;
They partly rise from angry thoughts,
  and partly from regret.
Regret—that spring comes suddenly;
  anger—it cannot last,
No sound to herald its approach,
  or warn us that 'tis past.
Last night within the garden
  sad songs were faintly heard,
Sung, as I knew, by spirits,
  spirits of flowers and birds.
We cannot keep them here with us,
  these much-loved birds and flowers,
They sing but for a season's space,
  and bloom a few short hours.
Ah! would that I on feathered wing
  might soar aloft and fly,
With flower spirits I would seek
  the confines of the sky.
But high in air
  What grave is there?
No, give me an embroidered bag
  wherein to lay their charms,
And Mother Earth, pure Mother Earth,
  shall hide them in her arms.
Thus those sweet forms which spotless came
  shall spotless go again,
Nor pass besmirched with mud and filth
  along some noisome drain.
Farewell, dear flowers, for ever now,
  thus buried as 'twas best,
I have not yet divined when I
  with you shall sink to rest.

I who can bury flowers like this
  a laughing-stock shall be;
I cannot say in days to come
  what hands shall bury me.
See how when spring begins to fall
  each opening flow'ret fades;
So too there is a time of age
  and death for beauteous maids;
And when the fleeting spring is gone,
  and days of beauty o'er,
flowers fall, and lovely maidens die,
  and both are known no more.

Now the handsome young prince and the beautiful young queen are no more. Only the solitary ruins of Craigmillar Castle remain!

ALLAN RAMSAY'S MONUMENT FROM WEST PRINCES STREET GARDENS

xviii
Reluctant Conclusion

There is an age-old Chinese joke about a man who was very fond of liquor. He could not afford to buy all he wanted, so he earned the drinks by telling people stories, at which he excelled. On one occasion he was being entertained in a house and his host became absorbed in the story he was telling. As soon as the man noticed this, he began to go into more and more detail, and although the story began to drag, his host's attention never wavered. Whenever the man reached a crucial point in the story, he paused and looked into his wine-cup. The host then knew that the cup was empty and called to his wife to fetch a fresh jug of wine from the kitchen. Each time the wife refilled the jug she dabbed a touch of soot from the stove on her face to record the number. Gradually the replenished jug took longer to appear, and at last the servant who brought it in lost patience and cried, 'For goodness' sake, sir, call for less wine and finish the story, or my mistress won't be fit to be seen!'

I very seldom tell my stories for wine, though I do enjoy a drop of Scotch from time to time; and here I send my thanks to the occupants of Cluny Castle, who used to spare some of theirs for me in the difficult conditions of wartime! Nor would

I dare to drag my stories out endlessly for fear my hostess or host might become unfit to be seen! Nevertheless, I do feel reluctant to conclude this record of my experiences in Edinburgh.

The reason is simple: I like Edinburgh. But I hesitate to state the fact thus baldly lest some day I meet a Glaswegian. I have always wanted to hear an argument between a native of Edinburgh and a Glaswegian about their respective towns, but though I have hopefully toured a number of little pubs along the Royal Mile, the pleasure has so far been denied me. One evening I was just passing Tron Kirk on my way to a pub near St. Mary's Street when I suddenly felt someone tap me on the back. When I turned round a man addressed me in pidgin English, a sort of Shanghai cockney, saying that he had been in Shanghai, Hong Kong, Amoy, Macow, etc. Obviously he thought that anyone from China would speak pidgin English, and probably thought himself clever to speak to me in the same fashion. His breath was strong enough to overpower the evening mist and he did not seem too steady on his legs. 'Come with me', he said, showing me two bottles projecting from his overcoat pockets. 'We can have a drink together.' I was touched by this unexpected friendliness, but not sure how to answer. 'I know your country', he continued. 'I am a citizen of the world. I am a Glasgow man. All Glasgow men go round the world. I went to your country when I was a sailor. Edinburgh pubs—no go, no go. Come with me. I have better drink.' I thought at once what an admirable opportunity this would offer me if I were to ask him to go into the pub with me instead. After a moment of hesitation, however, I decided not to do so, partly because there were wartime restrictions for aliens like me and partly because, after all, he might not have argued with the Edinburgh people. I thanked him very much for his kindness, and explained that I really did not drink much. 'Ay, no drinky? No drinky?' He laughed and went away.

Naturally not all Glaswegians are like this one, but a Glaswegian is certainly a man of the world. If he is not a sailor or a captain of a ship, he is a banker, a businessman or a colonising officer, who will certainly have visited at least one other part of the world besides Glasgow. I cannot afford to offend any Glaswegian. If I did, what would be the attitude towards me of his brothers, sisters, cousins, nephews and nieces in America, Canada, Australia, New Zealand and elsewhere? Then there are Aberdonians. Truly, there are good reasons why I feel reluctant to conclude by saying simply that I like Edinburgh.

On the other hand, I cannot easily contend that I do not wish to offend the people of Edinburgh by saying that I do *not* like their city. From my limited experience I know that these people are for the most part kind, tolerant and cautious. They would not take offence at my words, though they might try to console me by telling me to stay in Edinburgh a little longer and see more of it and that then I should certainly like it. And indeed there are many places in and round Edinburgh which I have not seen yet or which I have seen but not described, and I naturally feel reluctant to draw an incomplete conclusion. So I will briefly mention some of the other places I visited.

EDINBURGH CASTLE FROM THE BURIAL GROUND OF GREYFRIARS' CHURCH

I spent a whole day visiting Sir Walter Scott's house in George Square and the site of the old Royal High School of Edinburgh, and a number of other places connected with him. Then, though I care little for fighting weapons, I had a good look at Mons Meg in the Castle grounds. It is said that with the exception of a gun at Lisbon this is the oldest cannon in Europe. For one reason or another Mons Meg was at one time transferred from Scottish soil to the Tower of London. Scottish superstition declared that 'Scotland would never be Scotland 'till Mons Meg came hame', and through Sir Walter Scott's efforts it was returned to its original site, an act which would naturally help to engrave the name of Scott on the heart of every Scotsman.

I also visited Swanston Cottage, the country home of Robert Louis Stevenson. I went on a tram to Colinton and first had a look at the Manse, where someone had told me that Stevenson spent many happy holidays with his maternal grandfather. It was of this place that he wrote: 'Every sight and sound—the shadowing evergreens, the grey tombstones, the muffled roar of the water beneath, even the silence brooding in the churchyard above—conspire to feed a romantic imagination.' Then I was shown the way to Swanston. I do not know whether the road from the Manse to the cottage has changed since Stevenson's time or not, but I could distinctly hear the murmuring of the little river from Colinton Dell and this sound cannot have changed much. The green fields and pastures, the seagulls circling and crying over my head, were of all time. It was a lovely walk.

Lying as it does on the lower slopes of the Pentland Hills, the cottage was hidden in the thick foliage of trees. I looked over a fence and saw that the present occupants had tended the garden well and that flowers were blooming in the beds. I had no desire to go inside the cottage to see where Stevenson used to sit and sleep and have his being. I only wanted to feel the atmosphere of the place he had loved. 'The pleasure that we take in beautiful nature', Stevenson wrote, 'is essentially capricious. It comes sometimes when we least look for it; and sometimes when we expect it most certainly it leaves us to gape joylessly for days together in the very homeland of the beautiful.' As a boy Stevenson used to spend holidays at Swanston, and these beautiful surroundings must have provided him with a store of inspiration for his *Child's Garden of Verses;* I have read it with delight.

SWANSTON COTTAGE

I first came to know Stevenson through his *Treasure Island*. There is a Chinese translation of it, though not a very good one. It has never appealed to Chinese children as it has to British and American youngsters, perhaps because we have not much acquaintance with the sea. It does not seem to have occurred to the Chinese to go to sea in search of distant treasure, and no such adventures have been described in our literature. On the other hand, judging by certain English novels and American films about Chinese pirates, it would seem incredible that Chinese youngsters could not enjoy the spirit of *Treasure Island!* I suppose Chinese pirates are not great pirates but common robbers hugging the sea-coast, and only venturing on occasional small-scale attacks on helpless passenger boats. They have no organisation, nor are they ambitious to the same extent as Captain Smollett and others! To rob on a small scale is liable only to land one in jail; but large-scale robbery may lead to great honour!

Stevenson did not enjoy a long life, but his works have kept his name alive. He is without doubt a most worthy son of Edinburgh. He, Burns and Scott all rank among the great names of Scottish literature.

WATER OF LEITH

Another day a friend of mine, Dr. H. S. Peng, physicist at Edinburgh University, whom I happened to meet in the Chinese Restaurant in Chambers Street, suggested that we should go for a walk along the Water of Leith. He had been living in Edinburgh for several years and knew the place well, so I just followed him. First we took a bus to a quiet little village where there were a number of shops and houses but very few people. We rested in a field, gazing at the view of distant trees and hills, but the wind was too strong for us to stay long. We then walked down a long flight of steps leading through a lovely garden. About half-way down the slope we stopped, and I was surprised to find the place quite secluded. The trees and bushes hid the houses from our eyes. Peng led me for some distance along a narrow footpath from where we could hear the chattering of the Water of Leith far below. Presently we came upon some tall pillars supporting the huge arches of a bridge high above us. Near by an elderly man was dozing on a small chair, enjoying his midday rest, and three youngsters—one of them a girl in a red jumper—were clambering about on the rocks at the water's edge. It was very picturesque. We walked for a little while down below the arches, then followed the footpath back to the road above. I determined I would visit this delightful spot again, but so far have not had the opportunity.

THE MARTYRS MONUMENT

One morning, walking along Lauriston Place, I slipped inside the enclosure of George Heriot's Hospital, followed a path and presently passed through a gate into the burial-ground of Greyfriars' Church. I looked into the church and tried to read some of the names on the tombstones, but they conveyed little to me except that the church was very old; moreover, many of the names were illegible. This burial-ground, which has many grim, tragic and heroic associations, is said to be the most famous in Scotland. I read the wording

TWO SISTERS NEARBY SMOLLETT'S HOUSE

on the Martyrs' Monument, 'Of whom about a hundred noblemen and gentlemen, ministers and others, were executed in Edinburgh, mnost of them being buried here....' But have not similar events happened all over the world? Many human beings of past centuries have fought and sacrificed their lives for their principles. Many of us today have similarly fought and been sacrificed, and in all probability many yet to be born may have to fight and sacrifice themselves for their ideals. There seems to be no end to such struggles. Many Scotsmen must have stood in front of the Martyrs' Monument and felt grateful to those who died for the sake of their religion. The monument led my thoughts round the world and I mentally paid my respects to all who had died for their principles. Let us hope that some day we human beings will find a way of living at peace and with tolerance towards the differences between us. I should be glad to think that there will be no more martyrs' monuments, though the one before me, with the tall buildings and the Tolbooth spire of the Old City as background, provided me with a subject for a painting.

A visit to the National Museum of Antiquities of Scotland in Queen Street was a happy and memorable event. I looked first at John Knox's old wooden pulpit and one or two other objects connected with him; then at an exhibition of Scottish relics, of which two particularly appealed to me: one, a photograph of a Pictish cross, a slab picture stone with symbols, at Aberlemno-Angus; the other St. Vigeans, a stone bas-relief of a stag which struck me as very similar in structure and technique to our Chou (221–207 B.C.) jade-carving and Han (206 B.C.–A.D. 219) bas-relief. Professor V. G. Childe agreed that the similarity of some of the Celtic work to early Chinese art is very striking, but said he suspected a 'convergence phenomenon'. I expect he was right. I was interested that human beings, though divided by climate, geographical position and sea, should have approached art in a similar way. I am sure that we could all work together towards a common goal if we did not insist upon stressing our differences of race, creed, colour and culture.

Another morning I took my sketch-book and a little copy of Burns' poems with me to the Braid Hills. It was a beautiful day and I found that the Edinburgh sun *could* be very hot. On one side of the route there was a row of good, solidly built dwelling-houses which commanded fine views. After going some distance by tram, I continued on foot up a hill; I passed the road leading to the golf course and entered a narrow lane bordered with small bushes, mostly gorse. I went on and on. A few rocks jutting up here and there gave a jagged and unsymmetrical beauty to the landscape. I sat on several of them to make quick sketches of the distant views of Edinburgh Castle and Arthur's Seat. Looking through these scribbled lines and curves as I lay flat on the green velvet-like grass, I found them gradually changing into shapes of unknown insects and animals just as the scattered clouds in the sky were doing. I felt that none but I would interpret my sketches! My mind seemed unable to hold anything more; I began to feel drowsy and dozed. Then I opened the little book and read a few lines of Burns. I wanted to write something but felt too drowsy and I found that Burns had already expressed my thoughts:

> Again the merry month of May
> Has made our hills and valleys gay.

Certainly the 'our' should include me. He also wrote:

> Beauty, how frail and how fleeting!
> The bloom of a fine summer's day.

It made no difference to me that it was a fine summer's day in Edinburgh and not in my native Kiukiang. I felt completely in tune with him when I read:

> I'll be merry and free,
> I'll be sad for naebody;
> If naebody care for me,
> I'll care for naebody.

Here on the grass carpet of Braid Hills, naebody was bothering about me, nor I about anybody. Though I have always urged that we human beings should try to eradicate selfishness, yet I wanted to feel that at this moment Braid Hills belonged to me. A black-and-white sheep-dog roused me with his sniffing. He seemed to tell me that after all I was a stranger. I heard a call from the shepherd who was sitting on a distant rock with his flock of sheep nibbling below him. I could see him smiling, so I smiled back.

I have visited many other places in Edinburgh and there must be many more still that I have not seen, so my Conclusion must still be reluctant. The refrain of one of the popular Scottish songs offers me consolation, with its question:

'Will ye no' come back again?'

My involuntary answer always is:

'Yes, Yee will come back.'

THE SHEPHERD AND HIS SHEEP DOG